EXPERIENCES AND IMPRESSIONS-*THE AUTOBIOGRAPHY OF*
COLONEL A· A· ANDERSON

THE MACMILLAN COMPANY
NEW YORK   1933

Set up and printed.
Published June, 1933.

PRINTED IN THE UNITED STATES OF AMERICA
NORWOOD PRESS LINOTYPE, INC
NORWOOD, MASS , U S A.

PORTRAIT OF AUTHOR

WHENEVER A MAN
ACCOMPLISHES ANYTHING
WORTH DOING HE HAS HIS
MOTHER
TO THANK FOR IT.
I DEDICATE
THIS BOOK TO THE
MEMORY OF MY
MOTHER

INTRODUCTION

BY

THE HONORABLE EDWARD R. FINCH,

*Presiding Justice of the Appellate Division of the
Supreme Court, State of New York.*

HAVING read the manuscript and having known the author for many years in the close ties of friendship and of intimate acquaintance with his personality and character, I take pleasure in writing a foreword to his autobiography.

If more interesting men and women would write autobiographies, the world would be richer in helpful recorded experiences. For, after all, to measure what a human being has wrought into his personality out of the talents given him at birth, is one of the most educative and delightful exercises.

The month which I spent at Palette Ranch is a choice nugget of memory. The house which Colonel Anderson built, and which is more fully described in the autobiography, is indeed the conception and work of an artist. It is exactly in keeping with its purpose and setting. Easy would it have been to become a bit flamboyant. But no, just the perfect conception of a ranch house, situated on a rolling knoll with a view across the great plains and the rising, wooded mountains, out of which rushes the friendly stream, Piney.

But the personality of the owner interests me most. I had known Colonel Anderson in New York City as an artist, a well-informed man of the world, and one whom I found delightful company. But at Palette Ranch I discovered that he had sides to his character of which I had never dreamed. Here, indeed, in the ranch life of Wyoming he was truly at home. Here I found a successful rancher and a man who knew thoroughly his out-of-doors. Whether riding all day in the saddle or fishing in the Grey Bull River, making camp and cooking a tasty lunch or hunting, I found him equally well informed and able to do what came next to his hand. I have never seen a better marksman. But the part I enjoyed most of all was his companionship. Out of a wealth of experience, Colonel Anderson has evolved a philosophy of life and a practical knowledge which makes him a never ending source of delightful association to me. Here and there in the following pages his practical philosophy of life creeps in most interestingly, as "To make life endurable it is necessary to have a workable philosophy or a sublime faith." Again, where, out of a life-long intimate friendship with Thomas A. Edison, he quotes Edison as saying, while posing for his portrait: "No one can see and admire the wonderful laws of nature and not believe in a Supreme Creator." Or when he quotes the Indian Chief Washakie as saying, after General Grant had presented to him a handsome silver-mounted saddle and the Chief had refused to say anything even when the officer remonstrated with him: "The white man feels with his head; head has tongue. Indian feels with his heart; heart no tongue." And then when he quotes the woman with the hen who was the best hen mother in Wyoming, saying: "Give her a flock o' chickens an' they'll git brought up proper an' have good manners. I've lent her all over the plains, an' I git ten cents a head fer every chicken she brings up. That's some hen, my son. Ye got to take yer hat off to her. If human bein's would send the good mothers around the state to bring up the children—I mean them that knows how—we'd have better men and women in Wyoming." Then, too, there is Colonel Anderson's surprising practical knowledge which enables him, for example, to determine the points of the compass by removing the top of an ant-hill mound, the nest being always found in the southeast corner.

No one can think of Colonel Anderson and his many-sided interests, including his founding and maintaining for seven years, as President, the American Art Association in Paris, in order to succour the struggling American artists there, without being reminded of the wonderful work which his only daughter, Dr. Eleanor Anderson Campbell, is doing for thousands of mothers and children in the organization known as the Judson Health Center.

I have read the following pages of the autobiography with an added pleasure and interest because of my personal acquaintance with Colonel Anderson. The many who have a like personal acquaintance with him will, of course, enjoy the book most, but there is pleasure and profit sufficient in it for all.

CONTENTS

PART FOUR

PART FIVE

ILLUSTRATIONS

EXPERIENCES AND IMPRESSIONS

CHAPTER I

EARLY DAYS IN WYOMING

DEAR COLONEL PICKETT:

I understand you sent the sheriff into the mountains to arrest me. I presume it was because you were afraid of not getting back your small bag of salt which I borrowed, so I take great pleasure in returning it to you.

Yours truly,

A. A. ANDERSON

THAT summer I had planned a trip in the Rocky Mountains. I had left my studio in Paris for that purpose, and, a short time after my arrival in New York, I had entrained for Billings, Montana, where I was met by a man named Wolf, whom I had engaged as a guide.

Billings was a small town when I arrived there for the first time; the railroad had just been built to that point. As I left the train the morning of my arrival, I saw the body of a man who had just been hanged swinging in the air from a telegraph pole. He had shot and killed someone in the gambling saloon, and had been promptly lynched. The men who did it had no false modesty about the affair; they were lined up under the body, being photographed!

We procured a camping outfit at Billings and proceeded with our equipment to cross the plains, one hundred and fifty miles, to the foot of the Grey Bull Mountains. It was during the heat of summer, and across the dry alkali plain, at one point, we were obliged to travel forty miles without finding water. Approaching the foothills, we headed for the Grey Bull River and passed over a high plateau known as the Meeteetse Rim.

On this trail I met a Frenchman with a pack outfit. He had been up in the mountains on a hunting expedition and evidently had been quite successful in his quest for big game. As he spoke very little English, he was glad to converse with someone who knew his native tongue. When I asked him how he liked the country, he said, "Je n'aime pas un pays ou il n'y est pas le bons vin ni les jolies femmes." At that time, wandering over the wild wastes of Wyoming with but a few inhabitants, he was far removed from a paradise of that kind.

Descending the eastern slope of the Meeteetse Rim, we followed the trail to a log house that was a post office and a sort of grocery store, as well as a drinking and gambling saloon. It was kept by a Frenchman named Arland. I arrived at high noon and made the acquaintance of Arland. He invited me to stop for the noonday meal. Going through the barroom, he opened a door at the back of the saloon into the dining room. The dining room, with its bare log walls, had a table of pine boards in the center and a log on either side raised on four legs to serve as a seat. Seated at the table was a short, dark, bull-necked young man whom Arland introduced to me, saying, "This is Joe Crow, the best broncho buster in Wyoming."

I sat down and commenced my meal while Joe dilated on some of his experiences as a broncho buster. He told me how he had just been breaking a broncho for a ranchman. He said that the horse had fallen over backwards, breaking his saddle—"and the mean s— of a b— would not even pay me for the saddle!"

Having finished his hard-luck stories and his dinner, Joe Crow left the dining room. I soon heard the report of a gun. Joe Crow had got into a dispute with Arland. He pulled his six-shooter and opened fire. He shot off one of Arland's red locks of hair, put a hole through the sugar scoop, and kept on shooting, while Arland, in the meantime, was hunting for his gun behind the bar. He did not find it, but when Joe emptied his, Arland picked up a beer bottle and came from behind the bar. Joe Crow ran out of the saloon with Arland after him, and got caught in a barbed-wire fence, where Arland proceeded to knock him senseless with the beer bottle. Truly, I thought I had arrived in the land of the dime novel and of "gun play."

I took the trail up Grey Bull River and, after traveling for a few miles, I met a man on horseback who introduced himself as Colonel Pickett. I told him I had with me a letter of introduction given me by a friend of his in New York. The colonel had a ranch on the Grey Bull River near the point where I met him. He invited me to stop and spend the night at his place.

Meeting a man of Pickett's reputation was an event of some consequence. A cousin of the great General Pickett, he had been private secretary to Jefferson Davis,—but during the war he had fallen ill with camp fever. His doctor told him that he could live but a short time and, as Pickett was familiar with this portion of the Rockies, he had decided to spend his last days here. He recovered entirely, however, and lived to be over ninety years of age,—a fact that speaks well for the invigorating air of Wyoming.

Colonel Pickett had a large cattle ranch and a log house on the Grey Bull. We were served with a sumptuous dinner, and for the first time I had an opportunity to taste elk meat.

"I often wonder if we have any right to kill this noble animal," Colonel Pickett remarked, as he lay back in' his chair after dinner, picking elk meat from his teeth. "Of all animals the elk is God's most magnificent specimen."

It was common knowledge in the section that the colonel had been known to shoot this "noble animal" merely to see it fall and to test his own marksmanship.

The next morning I was packed up and was about to leave the ranch when Colonel Pickett came out and said to me, "If I were you, Mr. Anderson, I would not go up Grey Bull River. You are likely to get into trouble."

He then explained to me about a new law that the Wyoming legislature had enacted making it illegal for non-residents of the state to kill game.

"Colonel," I replied, "I am here more as artist than as hunter, and, if necessary, I will not kill any game. But in a country where game is so abundant and is constantly in sight, it is rather a hardship to be compelled to eat bacon. What would you advise me to do?"

"If I were you, I would turn back and go up Stinking Water," he replied.

This river is now called the Shoshone, but at that time it was known as Stinking Water; the Indians had given it that name because of the sulphur springs along its edge.

"But Stinking Water is in Wyoming, too!" interjected my guide, Wolf.

Colonel Pickett assented grimly. I saw he was not so much desirous of preserving game in Wyoming as anxious to protect the game about his own ranch.

"Colonel," I said, "when I hit a trail I don't turn back without a better reason than you have given me!"

I swung defiantly into the saddle and rode away, and, true to my declaration, my guide and I rode up the valley of the Grey Bull River, keeping our pack horses to the trail and camping wherever we found colorful scenes waiting to be sketched for my folios.

In this way, three months passed quickly, and I gave not much further thought to Colonel Pickett's injunction. But gradually the days grew shorter. The nights of occasional light frost were touching the leaves with colors, rich and tempting. I could no longer tarry; engagements in Paris and New York necessitated my departure. So we moved down the mountain once more, making camp late one day a short distance below Pickett's ranch, at a spot where the ranchmen were holding their fall round-up.

The plain, stretching before me as far as the eye could reach, was filled with thousands of cattle, some lying quietly, others grazing; while here and there was seen a cloud of dust raised by a small bunch of moving cattle. The scene was made picturesque and colorful by the Western cowboys, resplendent with silver spurs and trappings, broad-brimmed sombreros, and white-furred chaps, on their swift and some-times bucking bronchos. Occasional silk shirts of red and of blue, and gay-colored handkerchiefs loosely knotted about their necks, attracted the eye as the cowboys rode in and out of the herds, looking for and "cutting out" the brands of their owners.

I came upon a group of cowboys in time to witness a bit of excitement. They were standing in a circle inside of which was being staged a fight between a bulldog and a badger. The badger is an extremely pugnacious animal, and it takes a very courageous dog to overcome him. One of the boys, who was betting on the badger, thought he would be smart and, stooping down, patted the badger on the back. Quick as a flash, the badger jumped around and snapped off the end of the cowboy's finger.

That evening I was invited to have dinner with the cow outfit. Later, as we were sitting around the camp fire with a beautiful starlight night overhead, I told the boys of my experience with Colonel Pickett.

One of them, named Jack Stone, said: "Boys, let's go up and clean out the Colonel! He's encumbered the earth too long."

Some of the cowboys then told me that Colonel Pickett

had offered a reward of fifty dollars to anybody finding fresh game in my camp. Remembering that I had borrowed a bag of salt from him at the time of our meeting some months before, I wrote him the taunting letter that appears at the head of this chapter.

I was not satisfied with this gesture, however. His behavior continued to rankle, and presently I determined to take decisive action and to meet him on his own ground. Engagements in New York and Paris could wait, if need be. I would become a resident of Wyoming, if that was prerequisite to hunting.

I returned up the Grey Bull River and, ten miles above the Pickett ranch, I found a beautiful little valley. Beside the stream was a dense growth of cottonwood trees and, on either side, tall, luxuriant grass spread across the valley. An ideal spot, I instantly coveted it as a home. One hundred and sixty acres were quickly marked off, and at the land office I filed upon it a homestead claim. My guide was left behind to hold down my claim and with orders to build a small log house on the banks of the river among the cottonwood trees. Thus was founded Palette Ranch.

It is customary in writing a biography to commence at the beginning and record the different events of a life chronologically. But I am writing this book at my ranch, and I thought perhaps it would be well to welcome my reader here. I may not follow the traditional ideas of a biography, as it seems to me that what a man thinks, feels, and knows is as much a part of his biography as his acts.

Many things can occur between our first short gasps for breath and our last long-drawn sigh. I cannot recall them all, but such as I relate, I hope, will interest the reader, and, as we continue our journey, we will soon be calling each other by our first names.

PART
ONE

CHAPTER II

MEMORIES OF CHILDHOOD

"In childhood's hour with careless joy
   Upon the stream we glide;
With youth's bright hopes we gaily speed
   To reach the other side.
Manhood looks forth with careful glance;
   Time steadily plies the oar.
While in old age we calmly wait
   To hear the keel upon the shore."

As we sit in that calm tranquillity, memory at times plucks us by the sleeve and we see bright visions of our early childhood.

My earliest recollection is of being carried across a green field in the arms of my nurse in the bright sunlight. My father had settled at Peapack, New Jersey, and was building a home, a white house with green blinds, as I now see it vividly before me. The house was nearly completed and painters were busy inside. One of these workmen had engaged the fancy of my nurse; hence this journey we were making together to the new house. The front steps had not yet been built and there was a rough plank laid from the ground to the doorsill. I remember being carried up that plank and looking down, from what appeared to be a dizzy height, to the ground on either side.

We reached the doorway, and my nurse placed me on the floor while she went to look for her "soul-mate." With infant curiosity I crept about to investigate my surroundings. I found an open closet containing a pot of green paint. Green paint contains arsenic and is sweet to the taste, as I presently ascertained by popping some into my mouth. When the nurse returned and found me, I was covered with green paint outside and in, and only through the timely aid of a doctor with a stomach pump was I spared to make further discoveries. I have heard my mother say that this was where I got my first taste for paint.

In the next scene that appears before me I am lying on the floor on my tummy. Beside me is a box of water colors which my father had given me as a Christmas present. Before me is a volume entitled "Gordon Cummings Hunting Wild Animals in Africa." I am busily engaged in coloring, according to my infant fancy, the lions and beasts of the jungle. This may serve as a kind of omen, since the two ruling passions of my life have always been hunting and painting. I can now see before me a chubby hand, with rosy fingers and dimples, awkwardly holding a brush. It is hard to realize that that hand is the same as the hand that is now holding this pen. Ever since that time I have been busily engaged trying with form and color to reproduce some phase of nature. And many of my efforts have met with approval, perhaps not so much owing to their merits, as to the natural goodness and kindness of the human heart.

My early days were spent in "careless joy," and even now they echo across the stream of life like a ripple of laughter. I was fortunately born in a family where love was the dominant note. My mother had a family of ten children, but in spite of the conflict and strain that is natural in such a household an unkind word was never heard. Nine children grew to manhood and womanhood and, such was the force of my mother's moral influence in inculcating self-restraint and high principles, not one of the nine ever did an act that would bring disgrace on the family.

PORTRAIT OF AUTHOR AT SIX YEARS OF AGE
AND HIS BROTHER, WILLIE

The first sorrow and tragedy came into my life when I was seven years of age. I had a brother named Willie, two years my junior, a beautiful boy with golden hair and blue eyes and with, for his age, a very remarkable mind. At the age of five he could already spell many words, having had some instruction at home. He and I were inseparable. I have heard my mother say that when she saw one of us she never looked for the other, as she knew we would be together. One day my brothers, sisters, and I started out to gather chestnuts in an adjoining wood. We were running down a hill when Willie stumbled and fell. He struck his head on a sharp rock, fracturing his skull.

We carried him home, but in spite of all that science could do the injury proved fatal, and I lost my dearest companion. I now remember well the feelings I had the day that I stood beside the little open grave in the country churchyard where Willie was laid to rest. Few grown people can appreciate the deep anguish and sorrow that a child's heart can suffer. But in the buoyancy of youth we forget the despair that in later life follows falling tears.

A few years since, I visited this country churchyard and, on a marble headstone that marks the grave, I read these lines placed there by my father:

> God, in His infinite love, gave him to us,
> God, in His infinite wisdom, has taken him away.

At the time these words were inscribed I did not understand or appreciate them, but they reveal to my more mature mind the deep faith of my father, a faith that was his guiding star to the very end. To make life endurable it is necessary to have a workable philosophy or a sublime faith.

My mother said that I could draw before I could talk, and my fondness for drawing got me into my first escapade. I was about eight years old and was attending a day school in town. The schoolroom was a large auditorium with a raised platform at one end. The more advanced pupils sat in the main part of the room; on the platform was the teacher's desk; and behind it were some desks and seats for the smaller children. Being one of the youngest of these, I had a seat in the front row. Our teacher was a middle-aged woman of rather peculiar appearance. One day I amused myself by drawing a caricature of her on my slate, which set the children about me laughing. Without my knowing it, she slipped up behind me and saw this drawing. She was apparently greatly annoyed and grabbed hold of me, trying to pull me out of the seat. I held fast to the desk with one hand, and she struck me over the hand with a wooden ruler. I lost my temper, struck her with my slate, and then ran out of the school. Halfway home, I changed my mind, went back, opened the schoolroom door, and called the teacher all the vile names in my infant repertory,—some of them, I know, were a surprise to my fellow pupils. I then slammed the door, ran home, and throwing myself sobbing in my mother's lap told her what had occurred.

Mother, torn between love and duty, after kissing away my tears, told me that she would have to punish me. She produced a small whip and administered a few insignificant blows. I now know that this was not so much in the way of a punishment as to save me from a more severe chastisement later. My father was an old-school Presbyterian and did not believe in spoiling the child by sparing the rod. When he came home, my mother told him what had occurred, and that she had already punished me. Thus I was saved from an interview with a leather strap. Dear, gentle mother, who carried me under her heart and loved me before I was born!

I have already made some reference to a paint box I once received as a Christmas gift from my father. My first financial transaction was associated with this paint box. In my first ebullition of pleasure at receiving this gift, I took it to school and displayed it with pride to several admiring schoolmates. I then left it in my desk, from which it was presently stolen. I was much distressed, and I felt a special reluctance to tell of my loss at home for fear of being accused of carelessness. I, therefore, studied some way of replacing it. I went to my kind-hearted mother and asked if I might not collect and keep the old rags that had accumulated in the house. Old rags were in great demand at the paper mills, as the use of wood pulp in the manufacture of paper had not yet been discovered. Mother gave her consent. As soon as I had accumulated a sufficiency of old rags, I took them to the principal general merchandise store and exchanged them for eggs. These I brought to the drug store where my paints had been purchased and, after considerable juvenile haggling with the proprietor, I emerged with a happy heart, for I had exchanged my eggs for a paint box like the one that had been stolen from me.

It was at this period that my father reached an important decision. He had been well launched on a successful engineering career. He had been one of the principal engineers that built the Forty-second Street reservoir and also one of the engineers connected with the construction of the high bridge over the Harlem River. In his earlier days he had done surveying for the Erie Canal; in fact, it was while thus occupied that he had first met my mother. Now, however, he was strongly urged by his conscience to endeavor to aid the world by preaching the gospel of Christ. Accordingly, he had graduated from the Brunswick Theological Seminary and accepted a call to a small town in Illinois called Fairview. At that time Illinois was on the frontier, truly a part of the Wild West. There, for the first time, I saw the immense prairies covered with grass and wild flowers. Our table was frequently supplied with venison, wild turkey, and prairie chicken from the surrounding country.

While at Fairview, I continued my schooling. Like all school days, mine were a monotony of study and play, and I remember little worth recording. While I was in Illinois, Abraham Lincoln had his famous debate with Stephen A. Douglas in a near-by town. My father and my oldest brother, Calvin, drove over to hear him. My father came back an enthusiastic admirer of Lincoln, and remained his devoted follower and a staunch Republican all his life. Lincoln appointed my father a member of the Sanitary Commission during the Civil War, a commission devoted to the care of the sick and wounded soldiers. It was out of this commission that the Red Cross Society, known throughout the world, was formed. The red cross, taken as the emblem of the society, was associated with the career of Florence Nightingale. When she came back from the Crimean War, where she had instituted the first systematic relief for sick and wounded soldiers, she was decorated by Queen Victoria and given a beautiful pin, in the center of which was the red cross of Saint George. This furnished an appropriate symbol and name to the Red Cross Society.

I was still a very young child when, during Lincoln's presidency, my father took me to the White House to call upon him. When we entered the large room Lincoln was seated in an armchair beside a center table. He rose to greet us, and I see him now, standing before me, as distinctly as if it were yesterday; his tall, angular form dressed in black, his long frock coat, his black, tousled hair, dark beard, impressively rugged features, and deep-sunken eyes with their kindly twinkle. He shook hands with me and spoke a few kind words. I am glad to this day that I felt the warmth of the hand that signed the Emancipation Proclamation.

Christ died to make men holy.
He died to make them free.

While we were in Illinois, I received from my father the memorable gift of my first pair of skates. I was delighted with them and, in fact, was so proud of them that I put them on and wore them when I went to bed. It was then December. Bright and early next morning I set out carrying my skates and walked with a few boy companions to a pond about one mile away. There I put on my skates and, after some vain attempts, became so proficient that I was able to stand upon them. I then started across the pond. In the center I struck an air hole and went crashing through the thin ice. The water was over my head. When I tried to get out, the ice kept breaking away in front of me. My friends finally grabbed me and pulled me out on solid ice. I removed my skates and started for home. A cold north wind was blowing, and the thermometer was below zero. In a short time my clothes were frozen, and, when I reached the house, I was encased in a coating of shining armor. However, I did not suffer any ill effects from my polar experience, nor did it dampen my ardor for skating, in which I soon became quite adept, for I was able to execute the grapevine twist, the spread eagle, and other evolutions that appeal to boyish ambition.

Three times during my life I have been rescued from a watery grave. When I was fourteen years of age, I had a small sailboat and would occasionally make excursions from Flushing Bay to various parts of Long Island Sound. One day, while sailing on the Sound near Greenwich, Connecticut, I was overtaken by a violent thunderstorm. A sudden wind struck my sail and the boat capsized, throwing me out. I clung to the bottom of the boat and, in this precarious position, some distance from shore, was seen by members of the Greenwich Yacht Club, who sent a boat to rescue me. I was taken to the club, of which Boss Tweed was then president, and treated with the greatest kindness. I was furnished with dry clothes and a dinner, and, having righted my boat, I was enabled to continue my voyage on the Sound and of life.

We lived for three years in Illinois and then returned East, settling in Newtown, Long Island, where we remained for some years. I continued my schooling at the Fairchild Institute in Flushing, and from there entered the Grammar School of Columbia College. While I was living in Newtown, I had my first romance. A family named Warrin was among the town's most prominent residents. In this family was a pretty and charming daughter, Georgia. She had blue eyes and golden hair. As our families were acquainted, I often dined at her house, and we played games together. It was her feminine fascinations that first made my heart flutter. My youthful feelings sustained a considerable shock when she gave her hand and heart to another. A man may have numerous love affairs during his life, and many of these may pass completely from memory; but I doubt if the heart ever forgets its first awakening. There will linger a slight perfume, like the faint and far-away odor of mignonette. The memory floats before one like a strain of music from out the past.

Though I can trace my ancestry back to Philip Schuyler of Revolutionary fame, I do not think I will weary my reader with a chapter of "who-begat's," since it is more important to know where a family ends than where it commences.

My grandfather, Abraham Ryerson, and his wife, Sarah, my mother's parents, lived in Hackensack, New Jersey. I remember a large tree that stands in front of the house near the road, for the house and tree are still standing. My mother told me that she was at my grandfather's side when he planted it and that a man, who was riding by, stopped to tell my grandfather that Napoleon had just died.

I was born in my grandfather's house towards the middle of the century, and I spent many summers there in my early days. They have always remained a most delightful recollection. Frequently my grandfather would go hunting and take me with him. I was surprised to see him shoot squirrels from the tops of tall trees with a rifle of small calibre. I was allowed to carry the squirrels home, where my grandmother cooked them and served them, along with little fish I had caught myself in the stream running at the foot of the orchard.

The origin of the squirrel's name is interesting. A Greek philosopher one day was sitting beneath a tree, and above him, among the branches, he saw a squirrel sitting in the shadow of his tail. He named him σκίουρος, a compound of the two Greek words σκιά and ούρα, meaning "shadow" and "tail"; from this was derived our English word "squirrel," which means, "in the shadow of a tail." Of course the squirrel does not use his tail as a sunshade, but when he makes long leaps from tree to tree he does use it to guide his flight.

My grandmother had a beautiful garden filled with phlox, hollyhocks, and other old-fashioned flowers of the period, not planted in formal beds, but growing in the most luxuriant profusion. I remember seeing tomato bushes, bearing small red and yellow tomatoes the size of grapes. They were called "love apples," were considered poisonous to eat, and were only grown for ornamentation. The tomato, today, has become an important article of food. But my grandmother knew nothing about vitamins A and B.

While dietetics has only been studied seriously for the last ten years, scientists have found, after extensive research, that nothing we are accustomed to eat is injurious, and have recommended very few changes in our accustomed diet. The sense of taste in man and animals has always been a good guide. This sense of taste is aided by the sense of smell, particularly in animals. For this reason the nose has been placed directly above and close to the mouth, thus enabling animals to avoid any poisonous substance.

An illustration of the soundness of certain dietary customs is afforded by the Eskimos. When they kill a reindeer they eat the contents of the stomach. This does not sound very appetizing, but scientists have found that it is about the only article of the Eskimo's diet that is rich in vitamins. Wandering across the tundra, the reindeer selects a certain kind of gray moss and eats it; this moss contains a large quantity of vitamin.

Even before men knew anything about vitamins they were apparently as robust and many of them lived as long as at present. I had a great-uncle who lived to be ninety-nine years and nine months of age. I have always held a grudge against him for not sticking it out three months longer so that we could boast of having a centenarian in the family. But of this there may yet be some hope. The other day I called on a cousin of mine, Abraham Ryerson, who is ninety-one. He had just returned from calling on a neighbor three miles away, had made the journey both ways on foot, and, as evidence of a still youthful hardihood and vitality, I discovered him reading a book with the title, "Why Marry?"

CHAPTER III

AN ARTIST IN PARIS

I WAS desirous of continuing my studies and had some thought of making art my profession, but my father considered painting a rather Bohemian and unremunerative occupation and persuaded me to accept a position that was offered me in a wholesale dry-goods and manufacturing concern by the name of Libby and Company. I remained for a year or two in the dry-goods business, but did not find it very attractive. At that time the commercial use of rubber had not been made practicable and women, throughout the country, as a protection against rain, wore a waterproof cloak that was made from a fabric with a white cotton thread warp and black woof, altogether a gray and ugly garment. I conceived the idea of making a more attractive fabric with a yellow silk thread running up and down and, across it, a wool thread of a pretty shade of blue. It at once became popular and was extensively worn. Mr. Libby afterwards told me that the firm had made a net profit of $100,000 by its manufacturer and sale, a fact indicating that an artist's feeling for color can be useful in industry.

My brother Calvin was a physician and at one time I thought seriously of following in his footsteps. I even went so far as to study medicine for some months, though without entirely renouncing my commercial pursuits. During all this time, however, I continued to paint. I would get up at daylight and paint or draw until I was obliged to go down town. I did the same thing on Sundays and holidays. Moreover, I had made the acquaintance of Louis Tiffany, one of our best artists and certainly one of our great colorists. He invited me to work in his studio and I spent several months in these artistic surroundings, aided by his friendly advice.

Fortunately an event occurred that at last released me from my quandary about the choice of a career. Working at odd times I had turned out a picture that I called "Drawing Her Own Conclusions." It represented a half-life-size figure of a pretty young maid standing in her mistress's boudoir; under her left arm was a feather duster while, at arm's length in the other hand, she held a mirror, and in it was admiring her features. When this picture was completed, I sent it to the Academy of Design. The Academy of Design building was then at the corner of Twenty-third Street and Fourth Avenue. Here they held their yearly exhibition. My picture was accepted by the jury and hung on the line and received very favorable criticism from the various papers. During the exhibition it was purchased by an Englishman for the sum of $800. This success gave me so much encouragement that I gave up all thought of a commercial career and presently I also relinquished any thought of following the practice of medicine. I knew I would rather contemplate and study the beauties of line and form, as expressed on the outside of the human figure, than contemplate and study the diseases that might lurk within. Then and there the desire was born in me to be an artist. As soon as I could, I abandoned my other activities and set out for Paris to prosecute my art studies.

I sailed from New York on the White Star liner *Oceanic*. After an exceedingly rough voyage of thirteen days, we finally came in sight of England. What a thrill it was to see for the first time the green shores and chalk cliffs of that historic country, the home of my ancestors!

THE MORNING AFTER THE BALL

After a short stay in England, I went on to Paris, which was to be my home for the next ten years, and began seriously to study my art.

Paris in the eighteen-eighties! The time was when it was a pleasure to stand on the Champs Élysées as the golden rays of the afternoon sun poured through the Arc de Triomphe illuminating an avenue that was lined with chestnut trees in full bloom. Fine equipages, drawn by pairs of prancing high-steppers; on the boxes, coachmen and footmen in livery; and, in the open carriages, beautiful ladies dressed in chic and costly Parisian gowns, carrying bright-colored parasols as they wended their way to the Bois. Today the beautiful picture is no more. Now the Champs Élysées is crowded with ugly, honking automobiles and taxi-cabs, and the air is poisoned with the fumes of gasoline.

Some remarks of a contemporary French writer * will help to suggest the prestige that art and artists enjoyed in Paris at this time:

When all is said, it is the painters that are the glory of this epoch. Puvis de Chavannes is exhibiting his *l'Été,* and presently his *Sainte Geneviève,* those magnificent murals that give rise to polemics, generate enthusiasms and inspire the most violent attacks. But Cabanel, Bonnat, Meissonier, Dubufe, and Carolus Duran continue to paint in a style in which there is nothing extreme.

The newspapers of the day are filled with anecdotes about artists. They are fêted in the salons; they are put in the places of honor at fashionable dinners; they are universally run after. Great respect is accorded the petty foibles of such a one and the mannerisms of such another. People wish to become acquainted even with favorite models, the men and women whose lineaments some well-known painter has fixed on canvas—"for all time," as admiring ladies declare with a wistful sigh.

It is known, for example, that Bouguereau's female model is a cow-like creature to whom he pays a monthly stipend of three hundred francs, that she lives and eats in the artist's house, where she

* Jules Bertaut: "L'Opinion et les Mœurs."

spends her time knitting stockings in the kitchen. Whenever the artist requires, he sends out for her:

"Madame, demonstrate this position."

When he has completed his study, she goes back to her knitting.

It is known that Mme. Bertha, Stevens's model, is one of the prettiest women in Paris. Alive is Henner's model; she is destined to pose for his *l'Hérodiade* of the Salon of 1887. Adeline, nicknamed Mme. la Tetonnière, is Bonnat's favorite, while Aïcha, tall and frightfully cadaverous, boasts that she posed for Henri Regnault's *Salomé*. Clélie, who is thin as a fishpole, ordinarily poses for Meissonier. And this whole little group has its place in Parisian life.

On the left bank of the Seine, in the less aristocratic part of Paris, is the Latin Quarter, celebrated in song and story by Musset, Du Maurier, and innumerable other writers, as the place in which struggling artists have their homes and their studios, and as the residence also of medical and other students, whose Bohemian life adds color to that section of Paris. The Quarter contains many famous cafés, like the Café de la Rotonde, where tables are spread on the sidewalk; and here the students gather in fine black hats and vast neckties, loosely knotted, to engage with their models and mistresses in sprightly conversation as the glasses accumulate on the table and to spend a jolly evening in eating and drinking, singing, dancing, and discussing art, while pretty young girls, enhanced with powder and paint, sit at near-by tables, singly or in pairs, and on their faces, a look of invitation.

I established myself in the Latin Quarter and got down to serious work. Drawing is a matter of memory. You look at your model or at some object in nature; then you turn your eyes on your paper and draw what you can remember of the thing that your eyes have seen before looking at your subject again. Memory can be cultivated to a greater extent than any other faculty of the mind. In order to cultivate my memory I conceived the idea of reproducing during the evening at home the drawing that had occupied me during the day. I would work all day long in the atelier, drawing from the nude model, and then, after dinner, I would take a sheet of paper of the same size as I had been using and, with my charcoal and crayon, would try to reproduce my efforts of the morning. At the end of the week I would take home my drawings executed in the atelier and compare them with the work I had done at home. At first, the memory drawings contained many errors, but at the end of a month or so the memory drawings had become so complete and accurate that it was almost impossible to distinguish them from the originals.

I had thought at first of going to Cabanel's atelier, but finally entered the studio of Léon Bonnat, the most prominent portrait painter of the time. I studied one year in Bonnat's atelier, and then became a pupil of Cabanel. I later painted in the studios of Collin and Fernand Cormon. I modeled for one year under the supervision of Godin, the French sculptor, during which time I studied architecture, perspective, and anatomy by dissection. Later I rented a house and garden at Fonteney au Rose, a picturesque spot just outside of Paris; was a neighbor of Raphael Collin; and for two years worked out of doors under his instruction. Raphael Collin at that time was considered one of the best *plein air* painters in France.

Having completed my studies, I rented a studio in the Place Clichy, and commenced to produce pictures. Here it may be appropriate to introduce a few words with regard to the Salon. At that time Paris was the acknowledged art center of the world and had come to the apogee of its artistic splendor. The Salon opened every year on May 1st and was the most important event of the Paris season. It was thronged, not alone by artists and sculptors, but by men who were prominent in public life, including the President of the Republic, foreign diplomats, by distinguished visitors of all nations, and by everybody residing in Paris who made any social pretensions and was able to obtain a card of admission. Of course it was the ambition of every young artist to have at least one picture accepted and hung in the Salon. An artist, accordingly, would spend almost all the year painting one or two pictures to be offered to the jury. In order to be hung, a picture had to receive a majority vote. Something like ten thousand paintings were offered every year, of which two thousand, only, were accepted and hung. So long as the French government exercised supervision, the Salon continued to flourish, but when presently, under the Republic, the direction of the Salon was placed entirely in the hands of artists, cliques and quarrels developed. Instead of one yearly Salon, they now have five, and art has degenerated so that there is living in Paris today scarcely one great painter compared to those of the former period, and Paris has ceased to be the Mecca of art towards which formerly artists throughout the world turned their eyes, if not their steps.

My first Salon picture was a half-life-size figure of an odalisque lying on a divan surrounded by Oriental objects. I sent it to the Salon where it was received and hung on the line. My next important picture was called "The Morning After the Ball." It represents a life-size female figure seated in bed reading in the morning paper an account of her successful début of the night before.

This picture was exhibited at the Salon and more photographs of it were sold that year, according to my publishers, Braum and Company, who paid me a commission on their sales, than of any other picture in the exhibition. While in the Salon, it was purchased by Thomas A. Edison and is now hanging in his house in Menlo Park. He never allowed

"NEITHER DO I CONDEMN THEE"

it to go out on exhibition, fearful, as he has told me, that it might be damaged in transit.

The year after this painting was hung at the Salon a copy of the London *Illustrated News* was sent me, in which was a full-page illustration of the Czarina's boudoir in the Royal Palace at St. Petersburg. In the center of the wall was a copy of my painting "The Morning After the Ball."

The model who had posed for the painting was one of the leading *danseuses* of the ballet at the Grand Opera. She had a remarkably well-proportioned face and figure. After painting the picture I did not see her again for a number of years. One day, when motoring in the Black Forest in Germany with a friend, I stopped at the Stephanie Hotel and was taking dinner on the terrace. Imagine my surprise on seeing my model, beautifully gowned and still looking charming and youthful, seated facing me at a table only a few feet away. She was accompanied by a gentleman who wore the ribbon of the Legion of Honor in his buttonhole, and a child was seated between them who called her "Mama." She looked up and I could see that she recognized me; but she made no sign of recognition. Doubtless in her improved sphere of life she did not wish to recall her days as a model in Paris.

My next Salon picture was taken from the Bible story of the woman taken in adultery. The picture is some nineteen feet in length and is entitled, "Neither Do I Condemn Thee." Besides representing an episode in the life of Christ, the picture has as its motif the growth of the human soul. It is painted in three panels. In the first panel, the scene of which is at the entrance of the temple, the Pharisees are disputing among themselves how they may entrap Christ in his own words. The woman is being led by a slave, her husband pushing her, and a Roman centurion is keeping order in the crowd. Here, she merely shows anger at rough treatment. In the second panel, Christ, stooping, writes on the ground; the Pharisees, in hate, turn away from him toward darkness, but Mary for the first time realizes sin and turns to him in love. The scene of the second panel is the women's court of the temple. In order to make this correct in every detail, I had the background constructed of plaster in my studio and posed my models before it. In the third panel, Christ and Mary are alone; Christ is touching Mary's shoulder with a sympathetic hand and, as she hears our Saviour utter the gracious words, οὐδὲ σοῦ κατακρίνω ("Neither Do I Condemn Thee"), she looks up through her tears and sees a new life, new hope, and a new world.

Usually Mary Magdalene has been painted crouching on the ground in tears at the feet of Christ, who stands erect, towering above her, one hand raised in a preaching attitude. But while executing this work, it had been my idea constantly to paint the sympathetic and not the preaching Christ. I had just completed this third panel in which Christ's sympathetic attitude is especially emphasized, and the canvas was still on the easel, when I received a visit from the well-known artist Bouguereau. I asked him for his criticism. He passed some graceful complimentary remarks and then said:

"Mais, Monsieur! You have painted Mary not as a sinner but as a saint."

I replied with a question. "Is a saint," I asked, "a person who has never sinned, or a sinner whom God himself has forgiven?"

The purpose of art is to reproduce life truthfully. Art of itself does not point a moral or teach a lesson, but the influence of art on the individual is something, of course, over which the artist has no control.

In this connection I might relate an incident concerning the picture, "Neither Do I Condemn Thee." The summer after it was exhibited at the Salon, while on the way to my ranch in Wyoming, I presented a large photograph of it to the wife of the leading banker in Red Lodge, Montana. The banker's name was Meyers. I frequently stopped at their house in the course of my trips to the West. Mrs. Meyers had the photograph framed and hung it on a wall in her drawing-room.

The following year, in passing through Red Lodge, I called upon Mrs. Meyers, who at once said: "I would like to tell you an incident in connection with your picture.

"One day a lady of my acquaintance called at the house. I was in my room dressing, so I sent down asking her to wait and saying that I would be there shortly. When I entered the room she seemed somewhat embarrassed, had little to say, and soon left.

"A few days later she came to see me again and gave me her explanation. She said: 'When I came to see you a few days ago I sat for some time looking at that picture and was so impressed that it changed the object of my visit. I had come to say good-bye, as I was intending to leave my husband and go away with another man. But as I sat studying that picture I changed my mind. I went back to my husband, became reconciled, and am living happily with him.'"

CHAPTER IV

PAINTING FOR THE SALON

THE following year I painted for my Salon picture, one entitled "David Guarding His Father's Flocks." It represents a life-size figure of David, nude except for a goatskin thrown over the shoulder, standing with a sling in his hand; the sheep are crowding around him, terrified by the approaching lion. While I was at work on this picture, Samuel Clemens (Mark Twain), who was staying in Paris at the time, came frequently to my studio. I greatly enjoyed these calls, for he was quite as amusing in conversation as he was in his books.

When my picture was completed, I sent it to the Salon, and on varnishing day went there myself. Another picture hung in the Salon that year was called "Saint John Preaching in the Wilderness." It was a figure the same size as mine, likewise nude except for a goatskin. Saint John was standing with his hand above his head and two fingers extended pointing to the sky (they usually paint Saint John in this attitude although I never knew why). The first person I encountered on entering the gallery was Clemens.

He came up to me and said with his usual slow drawl: "I came here, Anderson, to see your picture of 'David Guarding His Father's Flocks.' I walked around till I thought I had found it, but when I looked a second time I saw it was Saint John hailing a cab!"

We walked through the different rooms, and I listened

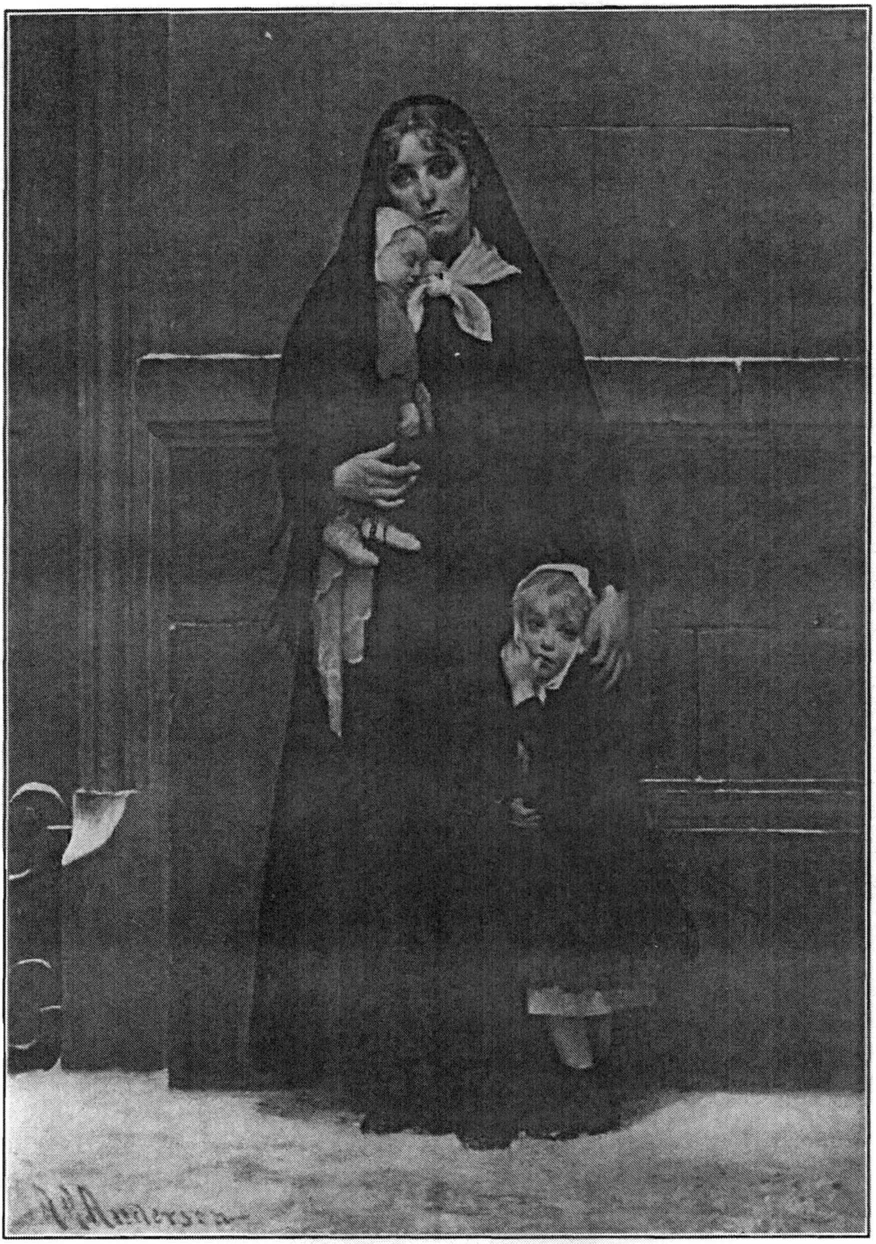

FROM RICHES TO POVERTY

to various other amusing remarks from the American humorist. One of these was, "There ought to be a Salon for literary works, and if there was Bret Harte would be hung on the roof!"

One of my Salon pictures was entitled "From Riches to Poverty." It represents a woman of evident refinement, but reduced in circumstances, standing in a snowy street holding a sick baby in her arms; another child, a little girl, is clinging to her side. This picture was later exhibited at the Universal Exhibition at New Orleans and received a medal. It was there purchased by the Merchants and Mechanics Institute of New York, and is now hanging in their rooms.

Having completed this work during the winter, I decided to spend the following summer in Les Andelys. Les Andelys was only a small, unfrequented French village at the time when I first went there, not the popular resort which it has since become. It is situated on the picturesque part of the Seine, just above Rouen, where the river loses itself in numerous islands. Carol Beckwith, a well-known American painter, and La Haye, a French painter of note, accompanied me. Beckwith and La Haye had their models with them. Our summer of sketching and painting was most delightful. Starting out early in the morning, we would look for a likely scene to sketch, never very difficult to find.

The village boasted but one hotel at the time. It was situated on the tree-covered banks of the Seine and it had but four rooms on the second floor. We rented it for the summer at the rate of three francs and a half a day, *tout comprit*. But after a short time the landlady, who had only recently been widowed, came to me with distress plainly written on her honest face.

"I find that I am losing money," she said, "at the rate I am renting these rooms, Monsieur. I shall have to raise the rent."

"That is quite all right," I replied. "How much more do you want?"

"Fifty centimes, Monsieur." She was still looking much concerned.

As those were not times of depression I agreed with an air of great generosity to a raise in rent that amounted to ten cents a day!

The inhabitants of this small village were mostly farmers. In driving and traveling over France, one sees few isolated farmhouses, as the owners of the land, guided by a strong social instinct, cluster their houses in a small village, usually consisting of minute, thatched houses directly on the street, with gardens in the rear. In the morning, taking their lunch with them, they go to their farms, which are cultivated by both men and women. After the day's work, the men gather in the cabaret to spend a social evening, smoking and drinking their light wines. This peasant economy allows each family a fair living, and the community life adds to the nation's store of happiness. France's ability to withstand the current depression is an evidence of the soundness of this economic system.

After our dinner, we often took a boat and, with the young ladies, glided out over the smooth, silken waters of the Seine. We all played guitars; so, with music and song, romance was added to many a moonlight night. We would return slowly, softly down the river, the stillness of the moon-silvered atmosphere broken only by the note of a nightingale in the trees overhead. But our life there was not all play. We returned to Paris at the end of the summer with a number of important canvases.

The two models that accompanied us that summer were ballet girls in the Grand Opera. They were not only beautiful dancers, but could sing beautifully as well. The following winter they went to Algiers for an engagement.

FRENCH DANSEUSE

While there they took a trip unaccompanied into the desert, and were captured and carried off by a band of Arabs. Days passed but they did not return. The French governor and the prefect of police at Algiers spared no effort to trace them; searching parties were sent out in all directions. But to this day no word has come back from them out of the white waste of the Algerian desert.

While at Les Andelys, I painted a portrait of one of the girls who were kidnapped by the Arabs. This picture may be seen in the following illustration.

In 1889, Paris held a Universal Exhibition, one of the most successful world exhibits ever given. I sent to the art department of the Exhibition a life-size portrait of Bishop A. Cleveland Coxe. It was purchased by the leading club of Buffalo and is now hanging in their room.

In one of the buildings of the Exhibition devoted to inventions, a large section was placed at the disposal of Thomas A. Edison. The Government conferred upon him the degree of Commander of the Legion of Honor. The Legion of Honor, which was first established by Napoleon, gives three degrees; Edison had previously received the first two. I was present at the elaborate ceremony at which the rank of commander was conferred upon him. When the French official handed to him a large diamond-ornamented badge, emblem of this order, he turned to me and said, "Anderson, they have raised my ante!"

Edison was constantly invited to receptions, banquets, and other formal social functions. But he was the most modest of men and did not care at all for these public events. Moreover, he did not speak a word of French and was very abstinent in his eating. One day he remarked to me, with a twinkle in his eye, "Anderson, I am never so happy as when I sit down to a ten course dinner between two Frenchmen who cannot speak a word of English."

The inventor was given a reception and banquet in the Hôtel de Ville by the city of Paris, at which Couptemps, the President of the city of Paris, said: "Paris, in the Hôtel de Ville, has given many notable banquets to emperors, kings, and other royalty, but this is the first time we have ever given a dinner to an inventor. However, in giving a banquet to Mr. Edison, we are giving it to a prince, as he is the prince of all inventors."

I usually accompanied Mr. Edison to these functions, acting as his interpreter. To avoid the crowd and find quiet, he visited my studio frequently, where I painted his portrait. I have never had a more interesting sitter. Like most great men, he was exceedingly modest, as ingenuous as a boy, and revealed a decided fund of humor. I painted him listening to his first perfected phonograph. Mr. Edison had been working a long time on the phonograph and had succeeded in bringing out every letter in the alphabet except the letters *p* and *s*. He was then striving for this result. He would repeat the word *specie* in the phonograph over and over again, making a record of that sound and then listening to the result. He sat up three days and three nights, practically without sleep or food, while his wife ran around with a sandwich in her hand trying to persuade him to take nourishment. At last the word *specie* came distinctly to his ear. He then considered his phonograph perfected. My portrait represents him at that moment. An historical picture thus resulted, showing the greatest of inventors listening to what he, himself, considered his greatest invention.

In Edison's biography by F. A. Jones is the following paragraph containing some record of my experience in painting this portrait:

Mr. A. A. Anderson, the well-known American artist, painted a very fine portrait of Edison in 1890. He relates some interesting facts regarding the inventor, and refers to Edison's attitude towards mathematics. He said: "I tried to paint Edison as a scientist, and it is the artist's duty not only to study his subject well, but to consider for what purpose the picture is designed. I enjoyed painting Edison although he is no easy subject. He is restless unless he gets his thoughts concentrated upon some scientific subject, and then he becomes quiet, and the expression on his face is one the artist loves to catch and transmit to the world; but it is not easy to get him thinking, for his brain works best in a noise. He likes to be in his factory or workshop with the hum and clatter of his machinery about him, but I know something about electricity and am deeply interested in it, so I was able by conversation to lead him in a train of thought that would get him into the proper condition to sitting as a subject.

"In painting him, I learned that he has the mind, not of a deductive reasoner, nor of an inductive reasoner, but the mind of a man inspired. He divines his conclusions by intuition, not by mathematical reasoning. For instance, when he invented the pear-shaped bulb for electric light, he wanted to ascertain its precise cubic contents. He gave the problem to several eminent mathematicians, of whom he has several in his laboratory, to figure out. When they brought him their result, he looked at it and said they were wrong. He could not tell exactly how he reached his own conclusion, but he knew what it was and wanted to prove it. His method of proving it illustrated the practicality of his ways. He made a series of tin cubes nesting inside each other, each a minute quantity smaller than the one enclosing it. He filled the electric light bulb with water and then, placing these different cubes on the table before him, he proceeded to pour the water from the bulb into first one cube and then another, until he found one of them which the contents exactly fitted. He then merely had to measure the length, depth, and width of that cube to arrive at its cubical contents. He placed the result in the drawer of his desk and allowed his mathematicians to continue their work on the problem until finally, ten days later, they brought him the same result."

I was delighted to have had the opportunity of painting the portrait of so great a man. I exhibited the portrait in the

Salon of 1890. The following letter from Dr. John H. Finley, editor of the *New York Times,* has fallen into my hands:

DEAR MR. EDISON:

I have seen today the remarkable painting of you and your phonograph made in 1890 by Colonel A. A. Anderson. It is quite the most interesting portrait of you I have ever seen. The "Wizard" in communication with the powers of light and sound here appears in the man.

Cordially,

DR. JOHN H. FINLEY

There has never been a more industrious worker than Edison. No detail was too small to be followed by him to its ultimate conclusion. The records of Edison's first phonograph were made on cylinders of wax. A brush was necessary to remove the small pieces of dust and wax that accumulated on the record. The only brush on the market at that time adequate for the purpose was a camel's hair brush that cost a dollar. Edison set about to find some hair from which a brush could be made that would serve the purpose equally well and be less expensive. He had specimens of every variety of fur from all the known animals sent to his laboratory. He required a brush in which the bristles were sufficiently long, with sufficient resistance, and with a point so fine that the wax would not be injured. After a long investigation, he found that the hair of the red deer met these requirements. It had sufficient resistance, and at the same time the point of the hair of the red deer is so -fine that it is difficult to distinguish even under a microscope. From this Edison manufactured brushes that cost only five cents apiece.

While Edison was sitting for this portrait, he was also working on the problem of the separation of iron ore from the ingredients with which it was mined. Up to that time the iron ore was separated laboriously by a complicated sifting process. Edison's fertile mind figured out a new method, baffling in its simplicity. His method was to grind the ore into small particles, which were then placed in a long metal hopper that had a narrow slit at the bottom running from end to end. Underneath was a receptacle with a metal partition in the middle; a strong magnetic current attracted the iron to one side while the débris fell on the other.

During one sitting Edison discussed the problem of the separation of iron ore with a man who at that time was the leading miner of ore in England. Later, as I ushered the gentleman to the door, he remarked, "Mr. Edison knows more about the mining of iron ore than I do myself."

While writing these words, the sad news of Edison's death comes to me. The world has lost one of its greatest geniuses and most interesting personalities. But millions of human beings today and in generations to come will be made happier and more comfortable by his wonderful inventions. Mr. Edison has been spoken of as an agnostic. That was not true. While I was working on his portrait, we had many discussions on metaphysics, and he told me that he believed in God.

"No one," he said, "can see and admire the wonderful laws of nature and not believe in a Supreme Creator."

He evoked out of the universe, electricity, and conferred on mankind the divine boon of flooded light.

CHAPTER V

TRIPS TO AMERICA

THE reader will doubtless have inferred from hints dropped here and there that my ten years of residence in Paris were interrupted by occasional trips to America, which enabled me to keep in touch with my relatives and friends and to form new association in the land of my birth. These continual crossings and recrossings afforded me many pleasant, or amusing, and some exciting experiences. Probably any man could fill a chapter with recollections of his narrow escapes from death, but such incidents tend to multiply in direct proportion to the extent to which a man knocks about in the world and becomes engaged in a life of action.

One of my very early trips across the Atlantic was especially memorable. I had sailed from Antwerp on a rather small vessel of the Red Star Line. A traveling companion on this voyage was the able and well-known American artist named Bunce, who had been living in Venice for some time and painting pictures of that colorful city.

"Sometimes," he once remarked in the course of a conversation about painting, "I let myself go and try to paint the worst picture I can, and the worse it turns out to be the better people like it."

Although Impressionism had not yet been born, this remark would apply to many of the pictures painted by the later school of Impressionism.

It happened that the captain of the vessel was also an

acquaintance of mine. I had made an earlier voyage with him. Accordingly, on this trip, I was seated at his table and some privileges not enjoyed by the other passengers were extended to me. On leaving port we headed into a storm, which continued to increase in velocity as we went farther west. I have crossed the Atlantic many times and encountered a number of storms, but never anything that equaled this one. It lasted the entire voyage, which took twenty-four days, and during that time there was not one day when passengers were allowed on deck.

Halfway across the Atlantic we met with a serious accident. The ship had a single propeller, connected with the engine by a single steel driving shaft. This shaft was made in twenty-foot sections and the sections were joined with flanges. The flanges were held together by bolts, eight steel bolts to each coupling. At the end of one section the bolts had been sheared away, so that there was no longer any communication between the engine and the propeller.

We remained in this desperate plight for seven days, drifting far out of our course. The vessel was equipped with a few sails, but the spread of canvas was not sufficient to enable her to make headway. The sails merely served to keep us quartered towards the waves and from rolling helplessly in the trough. Even so, the ship pitched and rolled with such violence that many of the passengers were injured; one sustained a broken arm and another a broken leg.

It did not seem possible that the vessel could roll so and again right herself. The tables in the dining room were fitted with wooden racks to secure the dishes and keep them from sliding about, a device which worked very well under normal conditions. But I remember one evening we had sat down at the table and hot soup had just been served, when the vessel gave a sudden lurch that threw both the plates and the hot soup over the passengers on the lower side of the table. Fortunately, I was seated on the upper side of the table and escaped the damage and the discomfort.

I also especially remember one evening being in the smoking room with some other passengers. There formerly had been several tables in the room, which were fastened to the floor, but these, like all of the furniture, had been torn away by passengers grabbing and clinging to them when the vessel lurched. About all that was left were a couple of benches against the wall on opposite sides of the room. We were sitting, or rather we were struggling desperately to remain seated, upon these benches, bracing our heels against a cleat that had been nailed to the floor in front of the benches for this purpose, when one passenger, a fat German weighing over two hundred pounds, was thrown from his seat and landed in the middle of the floor. A large copper cuspidor was skidding about and the German fell directly upon it, flattening it out like a penny. As the vessel continued to lurch from side to side, the German was flung back and forth like a shuttlecock. When he came over to the side where I sat, we would all try to grab him. But before we could get a firm hold, he would slide to the opposite side, and the passengers seated there would repeat our attempt without any greater success. It was some time before we succeeded in anchoring him and dragging him back to his seat.

The smoking room was on the top deck directly behind the bridge. I obtained the captain's permission to go out for an observation. There were steps just outside the smoking room, which led up to the bridge. I cautiously opened the door and, watching my chance between waves, succeeded in gaining the bridge. Canvas had been stretched all around the bridge to temper the violence of the storm, but there was a small crack between two of the strips of canvas, through which the pilot kept watch. I peered out through this opening. The wind cut like a knife. It was near midnight. There was not one star in the sky. Huge waves were sweeping the decks. The storm, apparently, was at its height. Dark, ominous clouds filled the heavens, and huge waves broke over the deck. It looked as though at any moment we might be swallowed up in the great maw of the deep. A more desolate scene could not possibly be imagined. I soon had enough and returned to the smoking room. It is fortunate that I chose that time for my exit, for hardly had I closed the door to the smoking room when the vessel was struck by a huge wave that carried away half the bridge and all of the lifeboats upon the port side.

A day or so later a sailor had a narrow escape. He was carried overboard by a wave from the forward deck. Luckily another wave brought him back and landed him on the aft deck. Otherwise he surely would have been lost, as no boat could possibly have been lowered in that raging sea.

These conditions had prevailed for a week, and the captain, who had to stay on the bridge almost all the time, was obviously very anxious. His face was the color of unbaked pie crust. One day I asked him to take me below with him to look at the broken connection in the driving shaft. He assented to my request. Although constant and arduous efforts had been made to repair the damage by putting other bolts in the place of those that had been sheared off, no success had thus far been attained, as the movement of the vessel kept the propeller revolving and frustrated every attempt. I saw the men put a steel bolt in one hole in the flange. It was instantly sheared off. I asked the captain to allow me to try an experiment. Being desperate, he assented.

I ordered eight bolts pared of hard, well-seasoned oak. They were two inches in diameter, not tapered but sharpened at one end. I had them placed in the holes, four upon each side, perforating one flange, but only just reaching the inside surface of the opposing flange. I placed four men on each side with hammers and instructed them to strike the oak pins simultaneously at the moment when the motion of the propeller brought the holes of the flanges into conjunction. The experiment was a success. All the pins went home and held. They were then removed, one by one, and the steel bolts were substituted and secured with nuts. When this had been done, the shaft was as good as new, and we went on our way rejoicing. Our provisions were almost exhausted and we were living upon short rations. The fresh water supply had been entirely used up; the passengers had to drink condensed steam taken from the cylinder heads, which tasted of verdigris, and was most unpalatable.

The storm continued, but we proceeded under a full head of steam, and on the twenty-fourth day of the voyage sighted land. While the seas were still raging, there was blue sky overhead for the first time:

> And torn white clouds the wild winds ride,
> Like shrouds of angels cast aside.

As at that day there was no wireless telegraphy our vessel had not been heard from during the entire voyage. It was long overdue and had been given up as lost, so that when I arrived a loving pair of arms, that were open and waiting to welcome me, received me as one returned from the dead.

During my early residence in Paris, I was taken with a severe attack of typhoid fever, followed by blood poisoning. I was kept on my back for three months at the Hôtel Maurice, Rue de Rivoli. I finally recovered, though reduced in weight to ninety pounds. At the same time my two brothers, George and Fred, living in New York, were also taken ill with typhoid fever and, to my great sorrow and grief, both died.

PORTRAIT OF BISHOP A. CLEVELAND COXE

As soon as I was well enough to get about, I decided to return to America to recuperate. I went directly to San Francisco, and there made the acquaintance of General Howard, who was exceedingly kind to me. He invited me to stop for a number of weeks at his home at the Presidio. While in San Francisco, I painted a portrait of General Howard, a life-size portrait of Sutro, Mayor of San Francisco, and also a large portrait of John Mackay of Nob's Hill.

Portrait painting has always especially interested me. The paintings that command the highest artistic admiration and also the highest commercial figure are largely portraits by Rubens, Van Dyck, Gainsborough, and others. Nothing can last unless it is founded on truth. When an artist is painting a portrait, he is obliged to tell the truth or it is not a portrait. Portraits, therefore, are apt to contain more truth and be more enduring than pictures which are mere figments of fancy.

In the course of my visit at the Presidio, General Howard was profuse in his reminiscences of the Civil War. This subject is one to which I have naturally given some thought, not only because of some boyhood memories of the period but also because in my later years I came in contact with a number of veterans of the Civil War and had dealings with them.

General Howard was especially eloquent and informative about the battle of Gettysburg. When Lee and his army left Richmond, they had two objectives; to carry the war into the Northern states and to capture Harrisburg, Pennsylvania, where large war supplies were stored. Lee had not premeditated a battle at Gettysburg but on more advantageous ground ten miles farther south. However, one of his generals, against orders, proceeded beyond that point and encountered at Gettysburg five thousand of the Union troops under General Reynolds, and a battle ensued. As he was losing in the conflict, Lee was obliged to send reinforcements until finally the main armies of both the North and the South converged at that point and fought one of the most desperate battles of the war.

During the battle General Howard, who was second in command, was standing towards evening, as he told me, in the belfry of the Gettysburg church. Through his glasses he studied the surroundings, asking himself, "What would I do if I were in command?" He decided that Cemetery Ridge, properly entrenched, would be the best point at which to repel an attack. At that moment an orderly rode up and saluted: "General Reynolds has been killed. You are now in command."

Immediately on taking command he ordered the troops to fall back to that point. The night was spent in throwing up fortifications on Cemetery Ridge. The next morning they were attacked by the Confederate forces. History tells of the terrific conflict that ensued.

The general told me an amusing incident that occurred at the beginning of the battle. He was standing in the cemetery when one of his aides said, "General, we cannot fight here!" and pointed to a sign nailed on one of the trees: "No Shooting Allowed." At that moment a cannon ball struck the sign and carried it away. General Howard replied, "Now that the sign has been removed, I guess we can continue to shoot."

General Howard with his force of five thousand held this ridge the entire day; that evening General Meade, recently appointed, arrived with the rest of the main army. The battle raged for two days more. On July 4, as a last resort, General Lee ordered the charge of Pickett's Brigade, which was as thrilling and desperate as the charge of the six hundred at Balaklava in the Crimea. This infantry brigade consisted of the flower of the Southern army. They charged across the open valley with unbroken ranks. As they advanced on the Union entrenchments on Cemetery Ridge, the general in command of the Union forces gave orders to his men not to fire until commanded, but to wait until the Southern army was at close quarters. Thereupon, at the command, they opened an intense cannon and musket fire. The charging brigade was cut down in a welter of blood. Only a small portion reached the entrenchments. A few crowded over the breastworks at the point now called High Water Mark. This was the turning point in the struggle for the preservation of the Union.

The Gatling gun was used for the first time at Gettysburg. It was one of the first rapid-fire guns ever made,— the precursor of the mitrailleuse perfected and used by the French in the War of 1870. At the close of the first day's battle, some prisoners of the Confederate Army were brought to headquarters to be questioned. As they were leaving, one of the prisoners saluted the colonel and said: "May I ask a favor? Would you please let me see that gun that you load up on Sunday and fire all the rest of the week?"

One day during my stay in San Francisco, while I was working on the portrait of Mayor Sutro for the city of San Francisco, Joaquin Miller, the "poet of the Sierras," came into my studio and was introduced to me by the mayor. I had read most of Miller's writings and poems and, in fact, had committed one of his long poems to memory. I recited it to him, and he seemed to be very much pleased that I was so familiar with his work. I saw much of Miller while I was in San Francisco, and I well remember one anecdote that he told me, which I set down as nearly as possible in his own words:

"One day when I was in Mexico I was riding through

a small Mexican village. It consisted of a single straight street with adobe houses on either side, in the doorways of which women were seated knitting and men were gossiping. Here and there was a muddy pool around which little children were playing. At the farther end of the street I saw an old colored woman coming out of a small cottage. She was grey and bent with age and shabbily dressed, and was carrying in her hand a small, broken flowerpot, tied together with a piece of string, in which she had planted a rose. She placed the pot on the step by the door and was tending it with such tender care that I stopped my horse to watch her movements. Not wishing to appear too curious, I addressed a few words to her.

" 'It's a very pretty evening, Aunty,' I said.

"The old colored woman straightened herself as far as her bent form would allow and, placing one hand above her eyes, gazed lovingly down the valley where the setting sun was projecting bright, golden rays, and trees cast their long, purple shadows, and said, 'It's a very pretty world, Massa. It's a very pretty world.' "

That old colored woman was a poetess and a seer. The story has remained with me, and whenever I see some especially beautiful phase of nature, I hear myself saying with that old colored woman: "It's a very pretty world, Massa. It's a very pretty world."

When I had fully recovered my strength, I left General Howard and other friends and returned to Paris, sailing on the same steamer with some artist friends, among them Billy Chase, Carrol Beckwith, and Fred Vinton of Boston. During the voyage we decorated the ladies' salon and painted a picture in each of the panels. My picture represented a young lady standing on the deck of the steamer waving good-bye with her handkerchief to friends on the pier as the steamer was leaving the dock. I have often wondered what

THOMAS A. EDISON LISTENING TO HIS FIRST PERFECTED PHONOGRAPH

became of these paintings, as some of them had considerable merit.

When we were a few days out, the birthday anniversary of Fortuny, a well-known Spanish artist, occurred. As one of our number, Blum, was a pupil of Fortuny we decided to celebrate the occasion with a special dinner. The party was enlivened by a case of champagne which Frank Hopkinson Smith had given us. During the festivities one of our members, stimulated by the champagne, grew sentimental and said, "Is it not astonishing how a little sentiment can make a paradise of a great waste like this!"

Another artist replied, "Is it not astonishing also how a little sentiment can make a paradise of a small waist!"

On our steamer was a friend of mine by the name of Collins. Collins was a member of Long's ill-fated polar expedition sent out to the Arctic by Gordon Bennett on the *Jeannette*. A few days after arriving in Paris, I was wandering through the salon when I saw Collins standing before a large painting of a polar scene by Bradford, representing a polar bear dragging some human bones from under a cake of ice.

"Collins," I said, "you are not contemplating a very cheerful subject. Tell me, what do you think of your chances of returning safely from the polar regions?"

"I think they are about fifty-fifty, but I am going all the same," he replied.

That was the last time I ever saw poor Collins. The *Jeannette* was lost and all on board perished. A year afterwards Collins's body was found by a searching party. It was evident that he had died of starvation, and in his last moments had been trying to eat one of his boots.

CHAPTER VI

THE AMERICAN ART ASSOCIATION IN PARIS

Not long after I had resumed my work in Paris, I was returning from lunch to my studio in the Place Pigale when I found in front of my door a handsome young American boy bathed in tears. I invited him into my studio and asked his troubles. There he gave me a pitiful tale of homesickness. He had come to Paris several months before to study art. He found himself in a strange city unable to speak the language. He had pursued his art studies for a time, but now found his funds nearly exhausted.

This was not an isolated case. I had seen many a young man similarly situated and from sheer loneliness drift into the most unfortunate associations. I decided that something should be done to ameliorate these conditions and, after long deliberation, concluded that a club or association might be formed where all the young American students and artists could meet and become acquainted, and be of some mutual aid and assistance to each other.

Searching for suitable headquarters, I finally found and leased, on the Boulevard Montparnasse, a fine, spacious house with large grounds enclosed by a high wall. The entire place was very much run down, but I repaired and furnished the house, and beautified the garden with plants and flowers. Then I called in the American art students of the Latin Quarter to form an association. The first night fifty young men were present. Then and there we organ-

THE TWO FIGURES IN BACKGROUND OF CENTRAL PICTURE ARE
WHISTLER, THE ARTIST, AND MISS ETHEL STODARDT, ONE OF THE
MOST INTERESTING AND ATTRACTIVE MEMBERS OF THE COLONY

ized the American Art Association, of which I was elected president.

I felt the boys would be more interested in the Association if they were doing something toward its support, so we decided upon ten francs yearly dues, equivalent to two dollars in American money. This, of course, did not begin to pay the running expenses, and for seven years I made up the deficit.

The Association soon had three hundred members and became one of the prominent features of the art colony of Paris. We had a good library, a reception room, a dining room where a student could get a meal for one franc, and a garden where he could find recreation and could sketch and paint. There were frequent social occasions, receptions, lectures and dances.

This was at the time when I had just begun producing pictures, and perhaps it would have been more advantageous to my art had I devoted my time entirely to painting pictures for the Salon. But for five years I gave almost my entire time to the Association, trying to help American art, as I felt that thereby I could do more than with my own brush.

There has never been any other American Art Association formed in Europe that lasted more than two years. That the American Art Association formed in Paris continued to exist until one year ago proves that it filled a need and was properly organized. During the many years of its existence, thousands of young American artists joined the Association and were aided thereby. When a young artist arrived, instead of being a stranger in a strange city, he went at once to the Association and was received by his compatriots, told where he could find board and lodging, and the best facilities for pursuing his art studies. He felt immediately at home; in fact, he had a home, where he *with best wishes for the prosperity of the Club, & still more for the prosperity & happiness of the President of the Club Whitelaw Reid.*

· MENU ·

Potage:
   Supreme et Jardinière

   Hors d'oeuvre

Entre:
   Vol au vent, sauce financière
   Filet de Boeuf roti, olive.
            pomme de terre.

Entremets:
         Petits pois, céleri.

· Rotis ·
Chapon roti, marmalade.
Salade d'endive.

· Desserts ·
Plum Pudding, Fromage.
Glace, Petits fours.

· Café ·

Complimentary to
THE HON · WHITELAW REID.

AMERICAN ARTISTS' ASSOCIATION

PARIS   MARCH 23
        1892 ·

could eat and pass the evenings in delightful surroundings.

When my affairs and interest made it necessary for me to close my studio in Paris and return to America, I resigned the position which I had held for seven years as President of the American Art Association, and was thereupon elected by the society to the position of honorary president for life. On leaving Paris, I was greatly exercised and concerned for the future interest of the Art Association, as to who would succeed me as President. My friend, Rodman Wanamaker, was residing in Paris at the time, representing his father's house, Wanamaker and Company. He was a particularly good friend of mine, and I usually dined Sundays at his apartment on the Champs Élysées. I finally persuaded him to accept the position of President of the Art Association. I had even more difficulty in persuading the Association to elect him, as they wanted Alexander Harrison or some other prominent American artist residing in Paris. But the members of the Association were not in a position to meet their financial obligations; so I doubted if it would continue to exist if they did not elect Rodman Wanamaker. This they finally did. He took a strong personal interest in its affairs for many years, and contributed large sums of money towards its maintenance.

To give a better idea of the scope of the Association, I will quote the following article by C. B. Bigelow, published in the *Graphic* in 1892:

The American Art Association, as the name implies, is composed of artists and art students of America who have made a niche for themselves in the famous "Latin Quarter." A club for American students was something needed, and several had been started, but they had all come to sudden deaths after brief and troubled careers. It was left for Mr. A. A. Anderson, a well-known American artist, to establish the flourishing institution of today. One day he noticed on the Boulevard Montparnasse a place for rent, formerly an old château; the interior was comfortable and, with few changes, well adapted for club rooms. There was also a garden, spacious and charming. Mr. Anderson rented the premises at once and, after fitting up the place, called a meeting of the students, and the American Art Association was organized. Mr. Anderson was elected president and has held office ever since, and has, with the greatest unselfishness, given his valuable time, his energy, and his money in founding and keeping up this Association. He remembered, when success and prosperity were his, the more vividly the hard struggles and trials which he had to pass through as a student. What indeed is a youth fresh from the United States and seeking an art education in Paris to do, ignorant as he is of the language and customs of the people, without aid, and, as a general rule, with the most meagre financial resources?

It used to be a very hard road for the student to travel, but today on arriving in Paris he can go at once to the "club" and become thoroughly posted as to ways and means. He feels at home; he finds himself among friends, congenial companions and surroundings, with those who are striving in the same direction, and who are absorbed in the great art world which he finds opened to him in Paris. In the reading room are to be found the latest and best magazines and journals, a good library and abundance of writing material, also chess and checkers, but cards and gambling are not allowed, nor a bar for the sale of liquors. Except during the summer months (when the majority are away on sketching tours) there is a restaurant on the premises for the convenience of the members. American holidays are enthusiastically celebrated. A wreath was placed on Lafayette's tomb here in Paris. A banquet was given to Minister Whitelaw Reid a few days before his departure for America; it was a great success and is numbered among the red-letter days of the Association. A series of receptions and entertainments are given during the winter, and monthly exhibitions of students' work. A prize of one hundred francs is offered for the best painting in oil or in water colors, or black and white, and one of fifty francs is offered for the best piece of sculpture or modeling in clay. The exhibitions encourage and stimulate. The students criticize each other freely, thus gaining knowledge through the interchange of ideas.

CHAPTER VII

WANDERINGS IN EUROPE

I HAVE always said that I preferred either the center of civilization or the center of the wilderness. In my frequent trips to America, during my periods of residence in Paris, I was drawn not so much to the larger cities of the eastern seaboard, which were growing increasingly noisy and dirty, as I was to the Rocky Mountains and especially Wyoming, where I was able to indulge my passion for big-game hunting. I made several early trips to Wyoming in the company of John Claflin, whose father was the most prominent wholesale dry-goods merchant in New York at the time. John Claflin was a young man of far more than ordinary ability, an honest, upright character, highly educated and with the highest ideals. My months of companionship with him had an influence on all my subsequent years. We found camping and hunting such a delightful and healthful occupation that John Claflin and I returned several summers in succession, while I spent the winters at my studio in Paris. These annual migrations resulted presently, as the opening chapter relates, in my acquisition of a ranch and of other interests in Wyoming.

This event, as I look back on it, appears more and more important. Paris, for reasons which I shall explain, was gradually becoming less attractive as a place of permanent residence. New York, at the time I established my studio there, gave promise of becoming an important art center. But that promise has remained to a large extent unfulfilled. Since the War things have taken a definite turn for the worse, so that in the modern world there is no place to which one can point as a center of civilization. Thus the ranch in Wyoming has become of increasing value to me, not alone because it has served as a refuge from a world in ruins, but also because it has been the means of my becoming actively associated with the material development of a vast area of new country which already supports a prosperous population and will one day become supreme as the vacation land of America. I was thus enabled to witness in some detail an important phase in the nation's history.

Before turning my back, however, as I presently did, on the studios of Paris and the art treasures of Europe, I should like to record some opinions and impressions acquired in the course of my studies abroad and my subsequent travels in Europe.

One of the marks which distinguish man from the rest of the animal kingdom is art. Throughout the immense period of human history and a great portion of the prehistoric period, art in some form has been practised by all nations and races, even by the most primitive savages. There is some innate impulse that inclines even children at an early age to try to draw. In the paleolithic period, some twenty-five thousand years ago, the Aurignacian man left specimens of his skill for us. This art work was executed on the rocky walls of the caves where he found shelter. In some respects these drawings excel anything that has since been produced. The artists represented deer, cave bear, the saber-toothed tiger, and other animals. They show a rapidity and sureness of touch since possessed by no other race. They saw the animal as a whole, and, therefore, no one feature exaggerated. Their quick eyes caught motions and poses that only instantaneous photography has since revealed.

From that period art continued to advance or recede, and at the Greek period, five hundred years before Christ, reached the highest point it has ever attained. It stands apart from traditions in its almost exclusive research for beauty, especially the beauty of the human form.

When I finished my art studies in Paris, I decided to visit Italy in order to study the great masters of the Renaissance. I took the train directly to Venice; that is, as far as the train went. At that time the train did not run into the city of Venice, but stopped at the edge of the mainland, and from there one entered the city in a gondola. That means of approaching Venice is far more interesting; running a railroad train into Venice is like taking a horse car to Heaven.

Venice, the beautiful city of the sea, resplendent with its blue sky, its dimpling canals, its stately churches and palaces, and its quaint houses with their window boxes of flowers. At times, peering from behind the flowers you will see a lovely face with flashing teeth and burning eyes, so attractive and alluring as to cause the holy men to grasp tighter their rosaries and mutter more rapidly the words of their prayers. Lovely, lonely Venice, lingering along its lagoons, sumptuously throned mistress of the Adriatic Sea.

The time of my first arrival in Venice was very fortunate. It was a glorious moonlight night, and as a fête was taking place the canals were lined with gondolas decorated with lanterns, and joyous songs with guitar accompaniments came from every quarter. With the glamorous moonlight falling on palaces and canals, one's Byronic dream of Venice is revived, a dream that fades unfortunately when Venice in its somewhat dilapidated condition is seen by daylight.

Venice has been called the courtesan city of the Renaissance. It has had a unique history, having existed for a thousand years as a nation,—longer than any nation in the history of the world except China which has been a nation for four thousand years, since the time of Genghis Khan. Venice remained so long a nation because of its isolated position, being, like England, largely surrounded by water. Venice was attacked many times, but was safe until long-range cannons were invented. The first soldiers that ever marched through her streets were those of Napoleon. Her downfall, however, did not come so much from force of arms as through loss of her commerce. When America was discovered and commerce extended over the Atlantic Ocean, Cadiz became one of the principal ports of entry and the wealth of Venice, which city up to that time had been mistress of the Mediterranean, gradually declined.

I was immensely pleased to visit this wonderful city and see for the first time the splendid Cathedral of San Marco, which remains to this day the most gorgeous and engaging example of taste in art.

Venice never produced any great poets, dramatists, or historians, but did produce some superb painters. The school of art in Venice saw its beginning with the Bellini family, father and son, the greatest of whom was Giovanni, although he has been excelled by his pupils, Giorgione, Titian, and later by Tintoretto and Veronese, who profited by his discoveries and carried them to a higher degree of perfection. I greatly enjoyed the time I spent before their wondrous canvases, with their glorious design and composition, and their glowing colors. All of them had something to say. Theirs were not merely blots of complimentary color put together, nor the rendering of texture and smooth surface like bits of still-life, as is that of many of our modern artists, whose pictures are as meaningless as the phrase, "Art for art's sake."

Painting consists of many things: drawing, composition, chiaroscuro, style, color, etc. No one artist has ever excelled in them all, but Titian came nearest. Since he did not excel in any one quality he is not considered as great an artist as Michelangelo, Velasquez, or Veronese. He was a most productive and energetic painter, and at the age of ninety he sent to Philip of Spain fifteen large canvases. He died at the age of ninety-nine.

From Venice I wandered on to Naples, a most picturesque city of great interest, but as this is not an Italian history but an autobiography I will not go into details regarding it. I went to Capri and saw the Blue Grotto, then to Sorrento, and across to Amalfi, which hangs on a cliff overlooking the sea.

A few years ago I again visited Amalfi to do some painting; but it rained constantly, so I decided to leave a short time after my arrival. When I awoke, the morning after reaching my decision, torrents of rain were descending. I hesitated to start out in this downpour, but finally got into my motor and pushed on. This turned out to be most fortunate, as that night there was an extensive landslide, which carried away and buried half of the hotel in which I had stayed.

I left Naples for Rome, the Eternal City, about which I had dreamed so much. Of course everyone knows that the gallery of the Vatican has one of the finest collections of art in the world; it contains canvases of the greatest artists as well as a connected history of art from the most primitive times down to a recent date.

The first night that I was in Rome I went to see the Coliseum. It was a beautiful moonlight night, so that my first view of the vast amphitheatre was most impressive. I saw where the Vestal Virgins sat, and thought of the days when on that same spot they had murdered Christians to make a Roman holiday. There is little left of the buildings of ancient Rome. The beautiful temples and palaces belonging to ancient times have been plundered by modern Romans in quest of material to be used in the construction of modern and less imposing buildings, leaving only bare brick walls that give no idea of their former beauty and grandeur. Even wonderful marble statues were burned to form lime. So today but little is seen that recalls the splendor of what was Imperial Rome.

St. Peter's, however, compensates one for such disappointments. When you walk across that spacious cathedral to the Sistine Chapel, containing frescos by Michelangelo, you feel infinitely small in comparison. One of the most beautiful examples of modern architecture is the dome of St. Peter's, designed by Michelangelo. Michelangelo was not only a great painter, but a sculptor, engineer, and poet. He was the last flower of the Renaissance. When Michelangelo died, art died like the century plant that, when it has once bloomed, dies to the very roots.

Having completed my sightseeing in Rome, I went to Florence. I would rather live in Florence than in Rome. There the wonderful palaces of the Renaissance are still in complete repair, furnished, and the walls covered with pictures of the period. The old and new parts of Florence fit in together so nicely that when you walk the streets you can easily imagine yourself five centuries back, and turning a corner you may hope to meet Giotto leaving his studio or Galileo coming down from his tower. Florence had the distinction of being the center of Renaissance art.

The first of her great painters was Giotto, born, according to Leonardo da Vinci, in the hills a few miles north of Florence. Here he spent the early years of his life guarding his father's flocks. He not only watched the sheep but constantly made drawings of them.

Cimabue, a noted painter of that time, saw by the roadside some drawings of sheep that Giotto had made on a smooth rock. He was so impressed by their excellence that he invited

Giotto to study with him in his home. Giotto's father fell in with the plan, and the young artist became a student of Cimabue, displaying unusual powers and making astonishing progress. He founded the Florentine School of Art and soon became not only one of the leading artists of Florence but also one of the greatest painters of his day. His works have seldom been excelled. The art school that he founded, continued and flourished under the patronage of the Medici family, a simple merchant family which gradually absorbed the government of Florence and became patrons of art and letters.

While modern Florence is one of the most interesting cities of Italy, how poor and drab it is when compared with the Florence of the Renaissance! Witty, gracious, and decisive by turn—*lo spirito bizarro Florentino*. With gusto and glamour and *bravura* they worshipped. With gusto and glamour and *bravura* they sinned.

Brilliant men lived in those days. There were architects like Bramante and Brunelleschi, poets like Dante and Calialanti, and painters like Michelangelo and Leonardo, all of whom caught some vision of beauty. Magnificent women there were, too, and their names are still familiar: Elizabeth Gonzaga, that poetess of pleasure; Victoria Colonna, who fascinated Michelangelo; and Lucrezia Borgia, made regent of the Vatican by Pope Alexander. Yes, these three, and also the versatile Tubia d'Aragon, loved by poets and nobles, and the adored and idolized Isabella d'Este—each of them a triumphant work of art, surrounded by pomp, beauty, and luxury. The leading artists designed golden ornaments for their coiffures and stunning jewels to adorn their bodies. They painted glorious frescos and designed rich brocades and tapestries to beautify the palaces where the favored Florentines lived in regal splendor. In no other country have artists received such high distinction as in Italy during the Renaissance. Here they were treated like princes, while in France a valet to the king was held in more honor than a court painter.

As Giotto was the first great artist of the Renaissance, so Cellini was the last. The night of his birth, his father, also a great artist, was walking up and down his room in anxiety. The nurse came to him with the new-born baby in her arms and said, "It is a boy."

"Benvenuto!" (Let him be welcome!) exclaimed the father, and from that day he was called Benvenuto. With the scintillation of his genius the last flickering rays of the Renaissance expired.

I have been very fortunate in arriving in many places at the right time without consulting the almanac or making any other special exertion. As I have said, my arrival in Venice was on a moonlight night. In the same way I saw for the first time the Coliseum. On my visit to Egypt I arrived at Karnak with a wonderful tropical moon making glorious the night, and thus for the first time saw its stupendous ruins. The same thing happened when I arrived at Granada, Spain; my first view of the Alhambra was by moonlight.

My travels in Egypt were accomplished with the aid of a yacht, which met me at Port Said. I remained seven months on the Nile, studying Egyptology. The ruins at Karnak are back in the desert, a short distance from the banks of the Nile. I proceeded thither in the manner that was usual at that time, on the back of a donkey. For some time I sat spellbound among the impressive and wonderful ruins, and my thoughts went back to the distant past when Egypt, for a period of five thousand years, had been one of the leading nations of the world. Since she left no written history, we know but little of her greatness, except that which we can decipher from her hieroglyphics, and what we see from the ruins of her wonderful temples and tombs.

Having finished my dream, I mounted the donkey and returned over the desert, lighted by a glorious moon, to my yacht on the Nile. On my way I passed through a small Arab village. As I was approaching this village, a large pack of dogs came towards me. In Egypt there are two distinct classes of dogs. Those of Cairo and Lower Egypt are medium-sized yellow curs without courage, the scavengers of the streets of Cairo, while the dogs farther up the Nile are an entirely distinct breed, large black dogs and exceedingly ferocious. Herodotus, in his history, speaks of these two distinct races of dogs, and says that while the dogs of Lower Egypt are without courage, those of Upper Egypt are larger animals and so ferocious that an owner, having been absent from his home for some time, does not dare return at night for fear of being attacked by his own dogs. It would appear that the same difference exists today. This pack of dogs came towards me in a V-shaped formation, a large black dog in the lead. As I felt myself really in danger, I drew my revolver and killed the leader, whereupon the others turned and fled.

For my journey in Egypt, I had provided myself with letters from the Khedive to the local governors. This proved fortunate in view of the excitement created by my killing the dog, for presently a delegation arrived before the governor in Karnak to complain of the act. I had presented my letter to the governor, and when this delegation arrived he was on board my yacht partaking of a glass of champagne. He was, therefore, in an amiable mood. He told the villagers that he recognized the justice of their claim, but he added: "Yesterday a Cook's steamer was here with a number of passengers, who also visited the ruins. (There had, in fact, been a large steamer of Cook's tourists at Karnak the day before, which, after visiting the ruins, had proceeded down the Nile.) If you will bring back this steamer and put Mr. Anderson among the passengers and then identify him as the one that killed your dog, I will see that you obtain justice."

This closed the incident.

From Florence, I went to Milan. I was greatly disappointed in Milan Cathedral, as it lacks majesty or proportion and is too ornate. But what I did see that appealed to me, that held me spellbound, was Leonardo da Vinci's painting of the "Last Supper." This great and wonderful masterpiece has unfortunately been injured by time and brutal restoration. "Intelligent" monks cut a hole through the center of it in order to make a door by means of which they could more quickly reach their dinner. It is still a work of art of the first magnitude, however. History tells of no man so supremely gifted for sincerity in his art as Leonardo. He was also a great sculptor, architect, musician, mechanic, engineer, and philosopher.

When Leonardo was a child, his father showed some of his drawings to Andrea del Verrocchio. This great Italian painter recognized their merit, and took Leonardo into his studio. Da Vinci flung himself into his work with the greatest ardor, and with a vision and insight never before shown by any painter. Unfortunately most of his earlier works have disappeared; nevertheless, some of the greatest treasures ever given to the world by the human spirit are embodied in his extant drawings, and the "Last Supper," the ghost of a picture, still indescribably impressive, will ever remain as a typical representation of that biblical scene. Another great work, now in the Louvre, is the "Mona Lisa," with her ineffable smile, as women then smiled, now smile, and will ever smile. It is a picture that, once seen, will ever haunt the memory.

After spending considerable time wandering around the charming lakes of Italy, I returned to Paris by way. of Switzerland. I am not particularly fond of Switzerland with its chalets and tinkling bells, and its hard colors of blue, white, and green. The people living in a country are usually about as big as their country, and Switzerland is one of the smallest countries in Europe. I have motored over most of Europe and nowhere have I met any trouble except in Switzerland. I had been motoring among the Dolomites, and on my return reached Ragatz, and then continued along Lake Zurich. I had proceeded but a few miles when I came to the town of Molls, a small town consisting of a few straggling houses and one single street. Entering the town, I found the road completely obstructed by three barrels with boards laid across them. A young man, who was sitting there in his shirt sleeves, looked at me without, however, saying a word. I thought that, on account of road construction, travel was being temporarily held up, and asked him what was the matter.

He came up to the car and said, "You are exceeding the speed limit."

I told him I thought I had been traveling very slowly. Whereupon he pointed to a small sign, barely discernible high up in a tree, which said that the speed limit was eight kilometers an hour. A man can walk faster than eight kilometers an hour, and it would be most difficult to drive a powerful car at that speed.

"Well," I asked, "what do you plan to do about it?"

"We are going to the Mayor," he asserted.

We started afoot up a narrow street, but had gone only a short distance when he told me that the Mayor was not at home.

"If you will give me one hundred francs," he said, with an air of concession, "I will let you go."

But I did not propose to submit to this obvious holdup;

so I got in my car, backed it around, and started in the opposite direction amid a shower of sticks and stones which the natives threw after me. When I arrived at a point about one-half mile below, I found the road completely blocked with another barricade, this one of logs. My coming had apparently been telephoned ahead and a reception quickly planned.

This time two hundred francs were demanded. Exceedingly indignant, I told them I would not give them one cent unless compelled to do so legally. Two of them got in my car and we drove back to Ragatz, where we appeared before a judge. The judge seemed sympathetic and said that if I would wait over till next day he would order a trial and investigate the matter fully, but if I was in a hurry and wished to proceed at once, he would name the lowest possible fine of forty-five francs. I was not anxious to remain longer in that part of the country, so paid my forty-five francs and started again on my way to Zurich, at the other end of the lake. Before setting out, I learned that the day before ten American cars had been held up in this way and forced to pay before they were allowed to pass.

I had in my pocket a letter from my friend Elihu Root, then Secretary of State, introducing me to all our ministers and consuls in Europe. So I called on the American consul in Zurich, presented my letter, and told him of my experience on the road. He promised me to take up the matter and see that I got my money back. He did investigate conditions and, after a lengthy correspondence, he informed me that no more cars were being held up at that point. But my money was never returned.

Unlike Switzerland, Spain has much of the natural coloring so necessary to the artist's craft. When I first visited Spain I went directly to see the Prado, one of the most interesting picture galleries in Europe. While the Prado is not a complete museum of art like the Louvre and the Vatican, it does contain many canvases of the greatest European artists painted at their best periods, many of them purchased by Velasquez when acting as Ambassador to Rome. The dry atmosphere of Spain is far less injurious to paintings than that of other countries, and the pictures there, without restoration, are in nearly perfect condition.

Spain has produced three great artists. The first of these was El Greco, who in reality was not a Spanish artist as he was born on the island of Crete. From there he went to Venice and became a pupil of Tintoretto, and then to Rome, where he studied the works of Michelangelo, and finally traveled to Toledo, where, for some reason or other, his art underwent a decided change. He then started to paint some of the most radical and stirring pictures ever produced, many of them great works of art. He was not appreciated in Spain at the time, died poor, and was buried in an unknown grave. As a matter of fact, he had scarcely been heard of as an artist until lately, when he was resurrected by the modernists to become their patron saint.

The best-known Spanish artist is Velasquez. He was truly a great artist; no one can help being impressed by his pictures. They are wonderful in color and painted with the greatest facility and spontaneity. One has the impression that Velasquez merely wished them and they appeared. They are largely realistic, and contain little of the spiritual quality of the works of the Italian artists. His large canvases left much to be desired in composition and grouping. He was eminently a portrait painter.

The third and greatest of Spanish painters, and by far the most powerful, was Goya. He lived at the time of the French Revolution, and was at heart a revolutionary and an anarchist. Inspired by the freedom of that period, he was a forerunner of a new freedom in painting. Although he painted many pictures that do him no credit, he also left many canvases that have been an inspiration to artists ever since. He produced some of the finest etchings ever made. Single-handed, he overcame all obstacles and made himself the foremost painter of Spain. Robert Henri, in his excellent book, *The Art Spirit,* says that in 1900 he met a French painter on the steps of the Prado. The great exhibition of Goyas had just been opened.

"Have you seen the Goyas?" asked Henri.

"Oh, yes," replied the Frenchman. "A wonderful genius. What a pity he could not draw!"

"He drew well enough to make you think him a wonderful genius," was Henri's quick retort.

This reply was witty but untrue. Goya was a great genius not on account of his drawing but in spite of it.

Since Goya, Spain has not produced a great artist. A Spanish painter named Zuloaga came to America a few years ago with an immense number of large canvases on which he had painted dancers, duchesses, bullfighters, laces, and fans. They were brutally painted, but he succeeded in selling a number of his paintings to rich Americans. His success, hard to understand, was due perhaps to his high-sounding foreign name. He returned to Spain and has not been heard of since.

From Madrid I went to Seville, one of the most picturesque of the Spanish cities, and while there saw eight bullfights in all their medieval gorgeousness. A bullfight in Spain, with the toreadors in their colorful costumes and the picadors on their horses under the bright sun, gives a most colorful, picturesque, and dramatic effect. In one bullfight I saw eight bulls, five horses, and one man killed. I commenced to paint a picture of a bullfight, but I became so disgusted with the cruelty of the sport, especially the maiming and killing of horses, that I abandoned the picture.

SPANISH–MOROCCAN STILL–LIFE

I also visited Granada, where I painted a number of pictures of the Alhambra. One night, after completing my painting, as I was seated on the top of the watch tower and from this high point enjoying the magnificent view of the valley of the Vega at sunset, the guardian of the tower called my attention to a small bridge some distance away.

He told me of the last call that Columbus made on Ferdinand and Isabella, then living at the Alhambra, where he pleaded for assistance in his contemplated voyage but was refused. As Columbus was sorrowfully leaving Granada, the queen, who was sitting on this tower, watched his retreating figure, relented, and sent a courier after him, who overtook him at the little bridge at which we were then looking, and asked him to turn back again. Columbus returned to receive Isabella's promise to assist him, even if she had to pledge her crown jewels.

The Alhambra, like everything that is beautiful in Spain, was built by the Moors in the course of their eight hundred years of occupancy. Although some of the Moorish art still remains, the Spaniards have done everything possible by their ignorance and superstition to destroy it, even going so far as to cover beautiful alabaster carvings with plaster. Charles V pulled down the winter palace of the Alhambra and erected in its place one of Spain's horrible structures. I heard a French artist say that he hoped the devil would burn as many zigzags on that monarch's damned soul as the decorative zigzags he had destroyed in the Alhambra.

The only republic that ever became an art center was Holland. It was a great art center at the time when Frans Hals, Rembrandt, and others were producing their remarkable works. But even these great masters were not appreciated by the citizens. Frans Hals died in the poorhouse, and Rembrandt, one of the world's greatest portrait painters, ended his life in poverty in the slums of Amsterdam.

Notre Dame de Chartres, erected during the reign of Saint Louis and inspired by Queen Blanche of Castile, who died in 1252, was built as a home for the Virgin Mary. No earthly queen ever had so regal a palace. It was built primarily by a woman to the memory of a woman, and you can feel a certain tender feminine touch throughout the whole cathedral. There are no pictures of bloody martyrs, or tombs, nor any tortured figure on the crucifix. The inspiring motive here is not fear but love. Everywhere throughout the church one feels the Virgin's presence and has no thought other than her majesty and grace. Her eternal instinct was to pardon, and her deepest passion pity.

Since the destruction of Rheims Cathedral, no other cathedral contains such beautiful glass as Notre Dame de Chartres. Stained glass is something to be felt, and no one now has the feeling for it that was had in the twelfth century. The finest stained glass that remains today is in the three lancet windows in the south transept of Chartres, especially the right-hand one representing the tree of Jesse. These lancet windows stand out at the head of all decoration, the finest in the world, as no other material, neither silk nor gold, nor color laid on with the brush, can compare with the effect of translucent glass.

If a digression is pardonable, it may be pointed out here that, contrary to the general opinion, there is no color in any object of nature about us. The sensation of color is produced entirely by vibration of light. The slowest vibration the eye can take in is red; the rapidity of vibration increases with the rate of the square root through the various colors of the prism until we come to the swiftest rays perceptible to the human eye, which are violet and blue. The

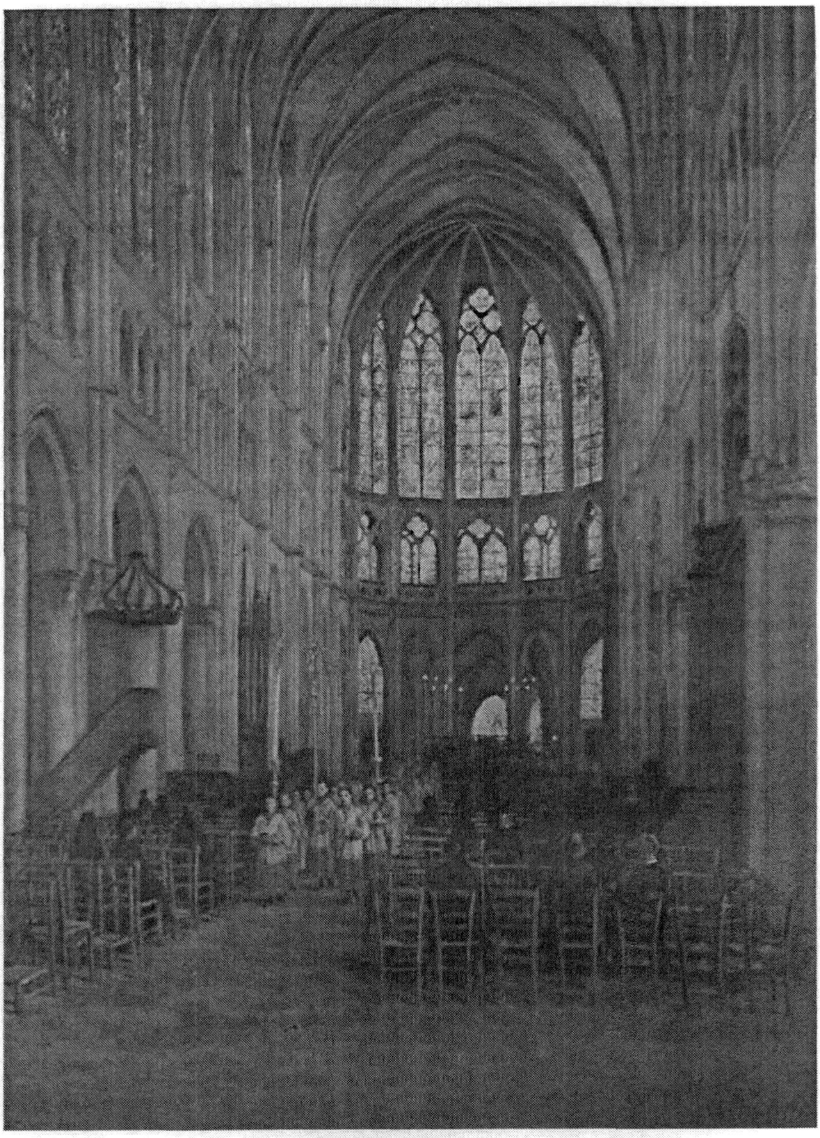

L'ÉGLISE SAINT PÈRES

objects about us contain various pigments that absorb certain rays of the spectrum and reflect others. These reflected rays impinge on the retina of our eye and are carried by the optic nerve to the brain, where they are arranged and classified under the names of the various colors. A red rose is not in reality red. It absorbs the green rays of the prism and reflects the red. If an object has color, therefore, it must be the color that it absorbs, not the one it reflects.

Since blue has the highest vibration rate, it is the most luminous of colors. To be truly beautiful, therefore, a stained-glass window should contain a certain amount of blue. The predominating color in these lancet windows at Chartres is blue, certainly the most beautiful blue I have ever seen.

For many years it had been my desire to make a painting of the interior of Chartres, but I did not find time or opportunity. Having some leisure, at length, I went to Chartres and spent three months painting the interior. I have never passed three happier months than those spent in the cathedral painting this picture. I worked in the cathedral directly from the original, a difficult task, since the only light received came through colored glass. When a morning's work, which had seemed to progress well, was seen in the clear light of out-of-doors, it was far from satisfactory. I could only work during the morning when the sun was on the east side of the church, and I was constantly interrupted by weddings and funerals. To occupy my afternoons, I also painted a picture of the interior of the church of Saint Pères, built during the same period. The hours passed, surrounded by the beauty of Chartres Cathedral, are among the most delightful of my life.

It is difficult today to realise the spiritual inspiration that went into the building of this cathedral. The large blocks of stone used in its construction were from a quarry five miles distant and were drawn to the cathedral by human hands. A thousand persons—princesses, nobles, and leading citizens—would haul on the ropes attached to the wagons of stone, interrupting their efforts occasionally to stop for singing and prayer. Arriving at the cathedral, they encamped about it and spent most of the night in religious devotions. These devoted hands raised the stones to build the cathedral walls. Truly spiritual devotion has never been more clearly exemplified.

When Chartres was completed, it was large enough to hold ten thousand worshipers, but still not large enough to admit the many faithful that crowded its doors. So greater room in the south transept was obtained by removing the outer wall and enlarging the transept forty feet.

Over the altar facing the south transept is a gorgeous stained-glass window, containing a large and beautiful picture of the Virgin Mary. For eight hundred years she has looked down in pity upon thousands of worshipers, who in anguish have come to her seeking relief from their sorrow. Today, seated there in this shrine dedicated to her worship, she looks down upon an empty church, lost faith, and a dead religion.

Men argue, dispute, and wrangle about dogma, creeds, and even scoff at religion; but when in some magnificent cathedral an immense audience of worshipers lift their souls and voices in songs and praise to the Supreme Being, mingled with the deep tones of the organ and heavenly voices of the boy choir that swells and vibrates through the arches, it is impressive, inspiring, and uplifting above small disputes.

PART
TWO

CHAPTER VIII

WYOMING CHARACTERS

THE reader will remember how, in my opening pages, I related the circumstances of an expedition that ended in my acquiring a ranch in Wyoming. The lynching at Billings, Montana, the fight at Arland's, the quarrel with Colonel Pickett about my killing game near his ranch were only a prelude, as it proved, to the drama of my life as a ranch owner in Wyoming.

That fall I had left my guide, Wolf, to hold down my claim and to build a small cabin upon it. When I returned to my homestead the following summer there was almost no grass on or about my ranch, not enough to support a saddle horse.

"What's the meaning of this, Wolf?" I cried as I pulled up my horse by the new cabin. "This cropping surely wasn't caused by drought."

"No, Mr. Anderson. Your neighbors, Colonel Pickett, Mr. Ashworth, and Otto Frank, herded five thousand head of cattle here all spring. I couldn't help it."

I sized up the situation at once and, as I had come there to stay, I decided to defend my rights.

Two of the principal factors in the settlement of the West have been barbed wire and bacon. There was one sure way to prevent the return of these obliging neighbors. I purchased a quantity of barbed wire, engaged more help, and enclosed my ranch, and, after I had obtained some more land, it was but a short time before I had a fence extending across the head of the valley from a high, rocky bluff on each side a distance of six miles, fencing out all trespassers.

And now, having a ranch in my possession, I decided I would become a cattleman. I bought twenty head of young Hereford cows and a bull, as a starter. The next spring they had nineteen calves, all but one heifers. This was fortunate, as I kept my heifers for breeding purposes.. In a few years, although I did not have "cattle upon a thousand hills," I did have a thousand cattle upon one hill.

One day, while working on the fence, some four miles below my cabin, I received an unexpected caller. He rode up to me and dismounted. Two six-shooters were in his belt.

"Are you Mr. Anderson?" he asked.

"Yes."

"Well, I am the sheriff, and Pickett says that you gave me a bribe last summer in the mountains not to arrest you."

His tone was belligerent and his hands were on his belt. We were alone.

"Now, look here," I replied. "You did not find me in the mountains and we have never met before today. So how could I have bribed you?"

He pulled a note from his pocket and handed it to me. It was written by Colonel Pickett:

Mr. Anderson told Mayor Wurstum, of Billings that he bribed you not to arrest him when you found him in the mountains. If I were you I would hunt up this man Anderson and settle the matter with him.

"Sheriff," I said, "Colonel Pickett is trying to make trouble between us and has given you a long ride for nothing. I will get you a letter from Mayor Wurstum saying positively that I never said anything of the kind, if you will then settle with Colonel Pickett."

My answer satisfied the sheriff, and I was left to continue building my fences. I had no difficulty in obtaining the letter from Mayor Wurstum and sent it on to the sheriff.

In order to add to the profit of my ranch I decided to try my hand at horse-breeding. At the time, at least, I thought it was for profit, but as I look back, conscious of how certain dark economic laws operate, I have decided that I raised horses for the fun of it. I went to Kentucky and purchased a carload of standard-bred mares and a noted stallion named Portculus, who had taken first prize that year at the Lexington State Fair. I shipped them to the ranch. It is an ideal place for horse-breeding. The high altitude gives the horses large lungs and hearts, and the dry soil, a small round hard hoof. The first thoroughbred came from the dry air and high mountains of Arabia.

Being naturally fond of horses, I was particularly delighted with the bunch of mares. At that time a fast driving horse would sell for as high as ten thousand dollars. A few years later, however, as the automobile began to replace the horse, I recognized the folly of raising horses for profit. Then, too, horse thieves were getting as numerous in Wyoming as the gangsters now are on New York's East Side. One night I had fifteen three-year-olds stolen; although I made every effort to trace them, I never saw them again.

At the time I first settled in Wyoming there was no law but the six-shooter. During the first seven years of my residence seven men were killed at Arland's, a gambling saloon twenty-five miles below my ranch, and not a question asked. Arland, himself, was finally killed by an unknown man, who shot him through the window of the saloon.

Many of the violent quarrels and shooting affrays of this period were connected with stolen horses. Shortly after I established my ranch in Wyoming I went on a hunting trip down the Grass Creek country, taking a small outfit and accompanied only by my guide. The first day I pitched my tent in front of a small grove of quaking asps. The next morning, leaving my guide in camp to attend to the outfit, I mounted my horse, and, with a rifle, started out alone in quest of game. I came across a bear track and followed it for some distance. It finally led up to the top of a mountain and then, crossing the divide, descended the opposite slope. Looking into the valley below, I noted a bunch of horses, and it struck me as very peculiar that I should see horses high in the mountains that late in the season. It was in the month of October. However, as I was a bit of a tenderfoot then, I gave the question no special consideration. I sat at the top of the divide for some time debating with myself whether I should follow that bear track any farther or return to the camp. As I was some ten or fifteen miles from camp and it was getting late, I decided I had better return.

The next day, with my guide, I went up the canyon above the camp. We had not gone far before I saw a large buck deer, which I killed. I left the guide to skin and to quarter it and made my way back to camp. My tent was pitched, it will be remembered, in front of a bunch of quaking asp trees. As I approached I saw a man cross the trail, riding in the direction of my camp. As I passed the bunch of trees I saw him dismount and enter my tent. I got off my cayuse, pulled my rifle out of the sling, walked up to the opening of the tent, and saw him with his back towards me, stooping down and removing my effects from a pack basket and placing them on the floor. I pumped a cartridge into the barrel of my gun but said nothing. He heard the click of the gun, put his hand on a six-shooter that was in a holster attached to his belt, and turned his head. Seeing that he was completely covered, he removed his hand from his gun, got up, and came out of the tent, saying, "I was going through your outfit, Mister."

"Yes, I am glad you told me," I said, "or I would not have known it. What are you doing here, anyway?"

"I am looking for some stray horses," he said nonchalantly.

He was a short, stocky man, with red hair, blue eyes, and freckled skin. And after a short conversation, as he did not seem particularly bellicose, I asked him to stay to lunch.

"No," he said, "no, I guess I will have to mosey along."

He mounted his horse and rode out of sight. My guide shortly returned and I told him what had occurred.

"I just met him," my guide replied. "His name is Sandy Martin. He is one of the worst desperadoes in the country. I'm surprised that there was no shooting."

It turned out that the bunch of horses I had seen on the previous day was stolen, and was being held in the valley by the thieves. Had I gone down and seen the brands on the horses, I might never have been allowed to return to report them. In one of Owen Wister's interesting books, he tells of some horses that were stolen in Wyoming and driven around the foothills into Jackson Hole. Their trail was taken up and followed by the ranchman who had lost the horses, who overtook them at Jackson Hole, killed all three of the thieves, and retrieved the horses. This is a true story. The bunch of horses that I had seen the previous day belonged to this outfit, and Sandy Martin was one of the thieves.

The state finally decided to give us a taste of justice. Wyoming was divided into judicial districts with a judge appointed to serve in each of them. The judge came to hold the first court in our district at the town of Meeteetse.

Nine prisoners were brought in, one a woman who had

poisoned her husband. When the judge came to hold court, he was, unfortunately, taken with delirium tremens. The district attorney was so drunk he could not lie on the floor without holding on. The two remained in that state for a week. The court was dismissed, and all the prisoners were turned loose. That was our first taste of "justice."

There was quite a noted character in that part of the country by the name of Sam Berry. A cowboy came in one day and said that he had seen deer meat in Berry's camp. Game laws had by this time been enacted making it illegal to kill deer at that season, and, as I was then assistant game warden of the state, I felt it my duty to investigate. I rode over to Berry's camp which was on Rose Creek, a small stream four miles from my ranch, and made a thorough search. But he had evidently been tipped off, as I could find no evidence of game.

Berry had just been pardoned from state's prison, to which he had been sent for murder. I sat talking with him for some time and as he seemed a pleasant sort of fellow I told him that I was about to make a camping trip in the mountains and asked him if he would like to go along as a horse-wrangler. He said he would. I engaged him, and the following day we started on a hunting trip in the mountains with a camp outfit and with Berry as horse-wrangler. I found him a very useful hand and interesting in many ways. I can see him now standing in the evening before the camp fire, balanced on one leg, and with one hand screening the firelight from his eyes, relating some of his interesting experiences. He would say, "When I was in the pen," as casually as another man would say, "When I was Senator." Berry remained in my employ about a year and we had no misunderstandings, although he got into very serious difficulties later.

I had working for me on the ranch a cowboy named Gallagher, the only man in my employ who ever threatened my life. Gallagher was a young man of twenty-four, handsome, six feet tall, splendidly set up, lithe and supple as a panther, one of the best horsemen and ropers I have ever seen. But his reputation was not as good as his figure.

One day he went to Cody, about sixty miles distant, and there got into some gun play, was arrested, and locked up. I heard of his doings, and when he came back I asked him what had happened.

"Oh, nothing," he said. "Only I captured the town of Cody and was about to trade it off to the Indians when they put me in the pen."

One day I was in camp by the roadside, and Gallagher was with me. Towards evening a man rode up rapidly on a horse covered with lather. Gallagher stepped up to him and said, "Look here, stranger, that horse you are riding belongs to me."

"I don't know nothing about that, but the sheriff is after me and the walking is all took up."

"All right, Mister. Go on," replied Gallagher.

He was sympathetic, for he, too, had had experiences with the sheriff.

At the end of the summer, I called the cowpunchers into my office to pay them for their summer's work before I returned East. When it came Gallagher's turn, I handed him a check for the amount due him. He looked at it and said, "This is not enough. I want seventy-five dollars more."

"For what do I owe you more?"

"I have been riding my horses looking for strays," he replied, "and I want seventy-five dollars more."

"Gallagher, that's all I owe you and that's all you'll ever get," I said.

"Mr. Anderson," he replied, "I will settle this with you the first time I meet you alone."

He went out with an oath, slamming the door. He never met me alone, however. A short time later he got into a dispute with a cowboy over a disreputable woman, and the cowboy, whose name was Miller, shot and killed him.

There were many vicious horses at that time in Wyoming that required great skill to ride. One day a man by the name of Fitch came to the ranch on horseback. He was a freighter by occupation, and he came to see if he could get an order to transport to the ranch some freight that I had at Billings. He remained for the night, and next morning, before leaving, came to the house, leading his horse, to bid me good-bye.

One of the cowboys said, "Stranger, do you know what horse that is you are riding? That is Dynamite. He is an outlaw."

"I can ride anything that has hair on it," Fitch replied, and threw himself into the saddle.

The horse gave a jump and a buck, throwing him and wrapping him around a pine tree. I rushed to his assistance and found that his leg was broken. There was no doctor within one hundred and fifty miles of the ranch; so I had considerable trouble transporting Fitch to a place where he could receive adequate medical aid.

Even in so remote a spot as Wyoming, there was sometimes a reflection of romance. A short distance down the river there was a large ranch owned by Mr. Morton, an Englishman. It was said that his father, in order to get him away from demoralizing influences in England, had bought the ranch and stocked it at an expense of two hundred thousand dollars for his son's reformation. Morton was an agreeable, well-educated Englishman. He lived on the ranch during the summertime, but, to escape his lonely surroundings, he went to Billings each winter. There he boarded with a lady who had a very comely little daughter about twelve years of age. Morton was greatly interested in this girl and sent her to England to be educated at his expense. She completed her education and returned an unusually beautiful and accomplished young lady. She made her home at the ranch with Morton and his partner, Jefferson, a handsome young Westerner. They both fell in love with her and there was considerable rivalry as to who would win her hand. Morton was a man in his early forties and of large wealth. Jefferson was penniless. A poet has said that

> Maidens, like moths, are often caught by glare,
> And .Mammon wins his way where Seraphs might despair.

However, after some hesitation, the young lady gave her heart and hand to the poor young man. They were married and continued to live at the ranch.

In the course of time Jefferson had to be absent on ranch business. He unexpectedly returned to the ranch late one night and found his wife in a compromising situation. But he did not take personal vengeance by shooting, in the Western style. Instead, he mounted his horse and rode to a near-by town, where he spent the night.

The following day he insured his life for ten thousand dollars, naming his wife as the beneficiary. He then went to Arland's gambling saloon and, wishing to disguise the motive for his intended act, he sat down at a table where some cowpunchers, among them my foreman, Rush, were playing stud poker.

He entered their game and played several hands. Then, drawing some cards for a new deal, he looked at them, threw them down on the table, exclaiming, "Oh, Hell! What luck!", pulled out a six-shooter, put a bullet through his temple, and fell dead against Rush.

On a high butte on the Morton ranch is now a single mound of earth, surrounded by a small picket fence with a headstone marking his grave. The last time I passed that deserted spot, a cold wintry evening, the lone gravestone was silhouetted against a starlit sky and all was shrouded in the mystery and stillness of night. In the distance the howl of a wolf sounded like the wail of some lost soul.

After Jefferson's suicide, Mr. Morton lost interest in the ranch and sought to console himself with alcohol. In a short time he died of delirium tremens.

Just above my ranch house there is a small stream called Jack Creek. This was named for Jack Bridger, who was one of the early pioneers in Wyoming and a man of unusual character. He once heard someone speak of a great poet by the name of Shakespeare, became interested, and asked others about him. He finally met a family who owned an edition of Shakespeare's poems, and as they were willing to sell the set, he purchased it. He could neither read nor write, so he hired a boy for forty dollars a month, a considerable sum in those days, to read it to him. He sat night after night by the camp fire listening to the words of Shakespeare until the last volume was finished. Shakespeare was a man of great imagination, but I doubt if he ever imagined that an illiterate man would sit all night by a camp fire in the solitude of the Rockies absorbing his writing.

After I had completed my house at the Palette Ranch and had it furnished, I asked Mrs. Anderson to accompany me on my next return to Wyoming. Although she was a little hesitant about visiting a country of Indians and wild animals, she did consent.

The railroad terminal at that time was Red Lodge, a point one hundred and twenty-five miles from the ranch.

Here our camp outfit met us, and the first night on our way to the ranch we camped on the Shoshone River near where the town of Cody now stands; at that time there was at this spot only one log cabin, which belonged to a man named Corbett. It was near sunset when we made camp, and we were about to partake of our dinner when we saw in the distance a cow outfit approaching. It proved to be a bunch of eight hundred cattle just purchased by Otto Frank, my neighbor, and was being driven to his ranch.

Mrs. Anderson was soon to realize that this was indeed the "wild and woolly West." The outfit camped on the river below us. After making camp and bedding down their cattle, two of the cowpunchers and a boy about fifteen years of age rode down to Meeteetse, the nearest town, and evidently spent the night in debauchery in the gambling saloons. At daylight they started back to the camp. The boy was riding ahead, and the two cowboys behind him.

One of them said, "I don't want that kid riding in front of me."

"All right," the other replied, "I will call him back."

"No," said the first. "I will do it myself," and he fired a bullet, hitting the road beside the boy's horse.

The boy came back!

Arriving at the camp at daylight, the cowpuncher called the cook, demanding, "Get up and get me some breakfast!"

The cook, a man by the name of Jackson, told him where he could go, saying he would get no breakfast at that hour of the morning. With that the cowpuncher fired a bullet through the tent. Jackson came out and the cowboy fired another shot that killed him, with the remark, "I guess I might as well clean up the whole outfit."

This, however, was prevented when a cowboy came out of his tent shooting, as they say. His first shot was fatal.

Thus in two minutes, two men had been killed. Truly a dramatic prelude to a summer's visit!

One bright Sunday shortly after our arrival at the ranch, Mrs. Anderson went out on the lawn and found Rush working there.

"Good morning, Rush," she said.

"Good morning, Mrs. Anderson," he replied, and added in his slow drawl, "I suppose, Mrs. Anderson, if you were in New York you would be going to church today."

Mrs. Anderson replied, "Oh, I might and I might not."

"I am very fond of going to church," Rush remarked.

"How long since you have been to church, Rush?" Mrs. Anderson asked.

"Just twenty-two years."

Had Rush received an education, he would have been a very remarkable man. But he had no education, and was scarcely able to read or write. He came from Kentucky and, at an early age, enlisted in the United States Army, entering the cavalry. He was with General Reno at the time of the Custer massacre, and, from the spot where Reno was entrenched, he could hear shots from the Custer battle.

An interesting story is my first meeting with Rush. I was hunting in the Grass Creek country and came upon the track of a bear in the snow, which I followed up the mountainside. I had my guide with me, and when we had nearly reached the top of the divide, I left him behind on the trail and went to the top. The bear is a nocturnal animal and usually does his traveling during the night. Often, when a bear reaches the top of a divide, he will lie down and hide himself in the brush and await the coming of night. When I reached the top, I saw he had crossed the divide on the run. I thought perhaps I had frightened him. I followed the track a short distance when I saw in the snow the footprints of a man following the same bear. As there was no sense in a double pursuit, I headed off in another direction.

When returning to my camp that night, I saw below me the smoke of a camp fire. As camp fires were few in that part of the country, I rode down to see whose camp it was. I introduced myself to the man I found there, and we had a short conversation. I was surprised by the neatness of the camp. He had tied together some willow branches, making a small broom with which he was sweeping up the ashes of the camp fire, a piece of neatness that I had never seen before. His name was Nathan Rush, and he so interested me that I engaged him to be my guide the following season.

This was the beginning of a friendship that continued for twenty-five years. He was my guide for several seasons and then became foreman of the ranch. A more faithful and brave man never lived. Several times he stood between me and death, and at any time he would have laid down his life for me. Like many Westerners, Rush at that time was rather a hard drinker. The habit grew on him until he finally became drunk. I then called him into my office and said, "Now, Rush, I think a great deal of you, and only one thing can come between us, whisky." Thereupon he signed the pledge and never again touched a drop of liquor, an indication of great strength of character in a man of his age.

One night Rush went to bed apparently perfectly well, but the next morning he was found dead in his bed, having died from a stroke of apoplexy. We placed him in a coffin with his favorite rifle beside him, and he was buried, sincerely mourned by everyone who had known him.

Wyoming has produced many remarkable men, such as Senator Warren, Frank Mondell, Senator Carey, and Governor Richards. The reason for this is that in the early days every man in Wyoming stood on his own two feet. Everybody knew just who and what he was. There was no need of pretence. If a man had ability and personality, the broad outdoor life of the frontier developed these qualities; if not, he went down and out.

Today all this is changed. The romance of the West has passed away. The frontier and the cowboy have disappeared, and we are all alike, leading the monotonous life of an industrial and mechanical age. Never again in the history of the world are we likely to experience the same kind of frontier life. There are no new continents to be discovered over which mankind will advance like a tidal wave, pushing before it a turbulent crest of white foam that ultimately settles into the still waters of civilized life.

CHAPTER IX

THE PASSING OF THE INDIAN

ONE time John Claflin and I were camping on the Crow reservation in the Prior Mountains. Our camp was well up near the top of a mountain at the base of which the Crow tribe had their encampment. They had built a corral enclosing their horses, and their tepees were in a circle surrounding it. The entire tribe was encamped at this spot.

One day I was riding along a high plateau when I heard behind me the pattering of horses' feet. I turned to see about one hundred Indians in their war paint coming towards me. I had been out of touch with civilization for three months and did not know if there had been an Indian uprising; I was, therefore, considerably startled, but, as they had seen me and I was in the open, there was nothing to do but continue my course. They rode up rapidly and surrounded me. One old buck put out his hand and said, "How!" I was greatly relieved to find his attitude friendly. They were a bunch of Piegan Indians. That night they went down to the Crow encampment, opened the corral, and drove off all the Crows' horses. The Crows may have heard them but they did not peep. The next morning, however, the Crows took up the trail of the Piegans and started in pursuit of their stolen horses, overtaking them at a point not far from our camp. Here they attacked the Piegans, killing one of them, and recovered their horses. This fight, that occurred so near my camp, was probably one of the last conflicts between hostile redskin tribes.

The Crow Indians have a reservation two hundred miles north of my ranch. The Crows have always been friendly to the white men and never have fought against them. Although they have aided the United States Army in many battles against hostile tribes, and have lost many men and horses in these battles, they have never even been paid for the loss of their horses, or have they ever received better treatment than other less friendly tribes of Indians.

The chief of the Crows was an interesting Indian named Plentycoup, whom I knew many years. Plentycoup was a very remarkable Indian and remained hale and hearty up to an advanced age. He became chief of the Crow tribe in 1875, when he was twenty-eight years old. Although he had assisted the armies of the United States in many of their battles against hostile tribes, the Sioux, the Cheyennes, and the Arapahoe Indians, and had had several horses shot from under him, his body bore only two marks: one, a scar on his chin where he was kicked by a horse, sustaining a broken jaw, and the other, a bullet burn on his neck.

The passing of the buffalo has changed the life of the Indian. As Plentycoup told me, "When the buffalo went away, the hearts of my people fell to the ground and they could not lift them up again."

When, as formerly, thousands of buffalo were roaming the plains, they were the Indians' principal means of sustenance. The meat was their principal food, and the hides made their robes and the coverings of the tepees. The Indians would remain on the government reservation during the winter and when spring came, against orders, they would leave the reservation and wander at will, often committing depredations on the white settlers. The passing of the buffalo made it impossible for them to leave the reservation and find sustenance.

You will often hear an Indian speak of "meat holes."

When the Indians killed a buffalo, they would dig a hole in the ground about three feet deep, would heat rocks, and would place them at the bottom of the hole. They would then cover the rocks with ashes and green twigs, and on these would lay pieces of meat. Then more branches, ashes, and hot rocks were added, and over the hole a green buffalo hide was stretched. The meat was left there during the night and in the morning was removed, deliciously cooked, and the Indians would proceed to gorge themselves upon it.

During many years spent in the West, I have been in contact with various tribes and have had an opportunity to familiarize myself with their characteristics and history, and the treatment they have received from the white man. As an evidence that most of the misunderstandings between the white man and the Indian are unnecessary, it may be remarked that, when Penn settled his colony in Pennsylvania, it was surrounded by various tribes of Indians; yet the Quaker settlements lived there for sixty years without any serious misunderstanding.

Our treatment of the Indians is a blot on American history. We robbed them of their land, killed them, and for years have practically held them prisoners on the Indian reservations. They have been changed from one reservation to another whenever the white men wanted their land. On these reservations they have been in charge of Indian agents who were often unscrupulous and dishonest.

Oil has been discovered on some of the reservations. From this source, and from the leasing of land for grazing purposes to the white man, considerable revenue has been realized. The money derived from these sources is paid to the government directly; then the government turns over to the Indian whatever amount it sees fit. But to this day the government has not rendered a financial statement to the red man.

Today the Indians are dying off by the hundreds from white men's diseases, syphilis and tuberculosis. Tuberculosis is an indoor disease; three hours of sunlight will kill a tuberculosis bacillus. When the Indians lived out of doors in their tepees, this disease was unknown, and it only became prevalent when the government built houses and forced the Indians to live in them. At the present time twenty-five per cent of the Indians are suffering from tuberculosis infection and scarcely anything is being done about it. The ill-treatment of the Indians has not been entirely the fault of the Indian Bureau at Washington, for frequently, when the Bureau has issued an order for their amelioration, Congress has stepped in and by some enactment has made it impossible.

About two hundred miles south of my ranch is the reservation of the Shoshone Indians, whose chief was Washakie. In recognition of some service Washakie had rendered during the Civil War, General Grant sent him a present of a handsome silver-mounted saddle. A large cantonment of United States troops were stationed on the reserve. The commanding officer, having drawn the soldiers up in line, presented this saddle to Washakie with great ceremony and a lengthy, grandiloquent speech. Washakie stood by with Indian stolidity all the while that the Colonel was making his address. When the Colonel had finished, he asked Washakie if he wished to reply. The chief shook his head, and declared he had nothing to say. The officer was disturbed at this seeming lack of response.

"What!" he said. "After all you heard the White Father say to you, have you nothing to say in reply?"

The Indian answered: "The white man feels with his head; head has tongue. Indian feels with his heart; heart no tongue."

CHAPTER X

THE YELLOWSTONE FOREST RESERVE

WHEN America was first discovered, no country in the world had more fertile soil or greater natural resources. At that time, New York State was a dense forest of white pine. But when the first settlers came, they started in to skin the country, taking everything possible out of the soil and putting nothing back. The first building put up in Rochester, New York, as in some other large towns, was a sawmill. Today there is scarcely a white pine tree left standing in the state.

The same thing has happened in New England. New England farmers, by their lack of method in the rotation of their crops and failure to fertilize, have so impoverished the soil that today New England contains hundreds of thousands of sterile, deserted farms. China is in many parts more densely populated than any other country in the world. Its entire population is sustained and nourished by agriculture. Yet the soil today is as productive as it was four thousand years ago, although no artificial fertilizer has been used; it has been kept so, in striking contrast to the sterile farms of New England, by proper cultivation and by putting back into the soil everything, including human and animal excrement, that has been taken out.

Beginning with deforestation, the wholesale slaughter of the buffalo and other game, wasteful methods of farming, the squandering of water-power resources and of wealth in mineral oil, the history of the country under white occupation has been a record of the heedless waste and destruction of our natural resources. But I will not weary my reader with more of this story than the part that concerns me, personally.

When I first went to Wyoming the government had not yet prohibited the free grazing of cattle on public lands. The possibilities and the necessity of a forest reserve were brought home to me by the fact that for two years I had not been able to see the mountains surrounding my ranch on account of the dense smoke from burning forests. It was evident that something more than mere coincidence lay behind the simultaneous burning of so many fires. I learned that many of them had been set by sheepmen, since it would be easier for them to trail their sheep through deforested areas, and since the weeds that would spring up next season were desirable food for sheep, which will eat weeds as readily as grass.

The extent of the damage that resulted will be best apprehended if we stop to consider that at the time of which I am writing, 70,000,000 sleepers were required every year to replace the worn-out and worthless ties in the roadbeds of our railways. Various substances other than wood, such as steel and concrete, had been tried but all had proved failures, as they lacked the proper resilience. Systematic forestry was necessary to supply this one demand for lumber if for no other reason.

But these forest fires were menacing in another connection. In Wyoming, for instance, all cultivation was, and still is, dependent on irrigation derived from streams that have their source in the mountains. The forest fires were bringing about the destruction not only of the trees but also the valuable spongy matter beneath the trees, so that the snow which fell during the winter, melting rapidly in the warm sunlight, was no longer absorbed but rushed down the mountainside like rain from a roof. Thus destructive floods in the spring would be followed by scarcity of water in the summer.

There was also the problem of wild game, in whose protection I had been interested for years. With the extinction of the forests the animal life was disappearing, and much of the indescribable charm of that Western countryside was being destroyed.

Clearly the situation was critical. A few wandering sheepmen were jeopardizing, not only the forests and the wild game, but also the prosperity of the farmers, the very life of the state. They were doing this at the expense of the local sheepmen, men who had a legal right to the home ranges. For the wanderers, bringing their flocks from the denuded ranges of other states after shearing time, could poach upon the ranges of the Wyoming sheepmen until the snow disappeared, and then could drive their flocks up into the mountains. They could keep the sheep in the mountains only about two months, however, and then they would again drive their flocks on to the home ranges of the Wyoming sheepmen.

These, briefly, were the facts that pointed to the necessity of some sort of forest conservation and control. Both economically and æsthetically the welfare of this portion of the Rockies was at stake. But what was to be done? State supervision seemed impossible; a great variety of factors opposed it, the chief of which was the fact that the lands in question were United States Government lands. The only solution seemed to be Federal supervision. I realized help must come from Washington.

I, therefore, went directly to Washington on my return East in 1901. Roosevelt was the first President to realize the necessity of conserving our natural resources. I had great faith in Roosevelt's personal interest in conservation, and I spent some months in Washington gradually arousing general interest in the project.

The wheels of government machinery, as always, moved slowly. Meanwhile, considerable opposition to my project had developed among Wyoming sheep owners. Although it was to their interest to coöperate, they had a mistaken idea of the probable results of the reserve. This was but human. The pioneer in any movement must often deal with opposition put in his path by those who receive the greatest benefit in the end. Matters came gradually to a head, however. After a lengthy consultation with the Departments of the Interior and Agriculture and others interested in my plan, I presented a tentative boundary of the reserve, which would include all the territory necessary, in my opinion, for the proper conservation of the vast tract of forest surrounding the Yellowstone Park. I then made a map of the proposed forest reserve and called at the White House to present it to the President.

Roosevelt's personal knowledge of conditions in the West made his early approval of my project seem certain. But his breadth of knowledge covering many fields is proverbial. I am reminded of the time I was lunching with Robert Bacon, our Ambassador to France, the day before Roosevelt was expected in Paris on his return from his hunting trip to Africa. In the Ambassador's office was a pile of books, among them Gore's "History of France", a twelve-volume work.

"Do you intend reading all these books?" I asked.

"No," he replied, "I bought them because President Roosevelt has written me that while he is in Paris he does not wish to meet politicians but writers, mentioning Gore particularly."

"Has Roosevelt read the entire work, do you suppose?"

"He has not only read all the volumes," Bacon answered,

PHOTOGRAPH OF THE AUTHOR WHEN SUPERINTENDENT OF
FOREST RESERVES

"but can reproduce whole pages of what he has read with amazing rapidity."

Roosevelt's astonishing knowledge of various subjects is well illustrated by the story which is told of his visit to the Field Museum in Chicago. He went there with a letter of introduction to Mr. Ayers, the President of the Museum. Mr. Ayers afterwards told me that he had taken Roosevelt through the Museum and had introduced him to the heads of the different departments, and that these heads of departments later declared that Roosevelt knew more about their subjects than they, themselves, knew.

As I have explained above, when I called upon President Roosevelt I took with me a map of the proposed forest reserve. I informed him that it had been seen and approved by the Department of the Interior and the Department of Agriculture.

President Roosevelt never took very long to decide any matter.

He looked at the map. "Anderson, do you think that's the right boundary?"

"In my judgment I think it is," I replied.

He immediately called in his secretary, Loeb, and in his terse way dictated a letter to the Secretary of the Interior, directing him to issue a proclamation creating a forest reserve following the boundaries furnished by the map. And upon formally presenting this letter, I had the gratification of realizing that the Yellowstone Forest Reserve was an actuality. Simultaneously, at the President's request, came my appointment to the post of Forest Superintendent, effective July 1, 1902.

CHAPTER XI

THE YELLOWSTONE FOREST RESERVE

(Continued)

ROOSEVELT thus officially created the Yellowstone Forest Reserve. My duties as Superintendent commenced at once. I accepted the position with the understanding that I was to be given full authority in all matters of organization and management. The reasons for this request were obvious; in this vast and wild tract of land, so far removed from Washington, any rapid communication with the authorities in the capital would have been impossible. There had to be someone on the spot who could act quickly and with full power. Consequently I was given complete control, my jurisdiction extending over such privileges as the making of all appointments and promotion within the Reserve, the issue of grazing and timber permits, the surveying of the boundaries, and reporting to Washington what had been done.

The surveying of the boundaries alone was no small undertaking, for it necessitated the work of a party of ten men with thirty-five saddle and pack horses over a period of three months, with a moving of camp almost every day. But the work was a privilege, and it was a satisfaction to know that the government was behind the project.

When surveying and laying out the southern boundary of the Yellowstone Forest Reserve, I camped one night at a cantonment of United States soldiers. Late in the afternoon, as I was talking to the commander of the post, a covered wagon drove up. In the wagon were a man, his wife, a little girl, and their household goods. The man came forward and said their little boy had died two days before and, as they did not want to leave him alone on the open prairie, they had driven to the cantonment to ask if they might bury him there. Permission being given, they made a rude coffin of pine boards, dug a grave, and in the twilight laid him to rest.

Early the next morning, as they were ready to depart, I saw the little girl coming into camp with her arms full of wild flowers she had gathered; she placed them on her little brother's grave, and they continued their sorrowful journey.

When the survey had been finished, and the exact boundaries of the Reserve had been ascertained and marked, my next concern was about the judicious appointment of a group of executives and assistants to enforce all rules and regulations. I divided the territory into four divisions, north, east, south, and west of the park, known as the Shoshone, Absaroka, Teton, and Wind River divisions. The divisions were then broken up into ranges with a ranger in charge of each. The rangers were obliged to report facts of importance to the supervisor, who submitted reports to me every two weeks. Thus was I able to keep in touch with all important developments and to forward my own reports to Washington. In passing, it may be remarked that these are the fundamental principles of organization which, due to their effectiveness and the facility of their operation, have been more or less applied to every forest reserve which has since been created.

When the Reserve was first organized every paper in Wyoming except one—and that one I owned—attacked me most severely. To read their articles one would think that

I had horns and hoofs. To give an example of their caustic criticism, I quote from the *Meeteetse News:*

Mr. Anderson can, by a single stroke of his diamond-bedecked hand, put out of existence that noble animal (the sheep) that clothes his unclean body.

Though the work of the Reserve was now going forward, its benefits naturally could not be fully realized at the outset. The resentment of the sheepmen continued to smoulder, and in several instances actually burst into flame.

The sheepmen seemed to consider the Reserve an attack on their special interests and began holding meetings at various places. One of these meetings was held at Meeteetse, Wyoming, and, happening to hear about it beforehand, I determined to attend it myself. In an upper room over a saloon, I found one hundred and twenty-five sheepmen gathered with the intention of arousing resentment against the Reserve. At my entrance the excited buzzing of the many voices ceased. I could sense hostility in the atmosphere, which in a moment was crystallized into someone's suggesting the advisability of a rope! My situation was ticklish, for most of the men were armed, some of them under the influence of liquor, and all of them belligerent.

Fortunately for me, the chairman of the meeting, Governor George Beck, a man who was not in the sheep business himself, met the emergency by remarking, "I see that Mr. Anderson, the Superintendent of the Reserve, is in our midst. I'd like to call on him for a few remarks."

This was just the opportunity I desired. I gave my views regarding the Reserve, and told them straight from the shoulder why I considered their present attitude mistaken. I explained how, instead of harming Wyoming sheepmen, the Reserve would be of inestimable value to them; for in that part of the land that was taken from the state of Wyoming, grazing permits would be given only to residents of the state. Thus their home ranges would be unmolested by wandering herds from other states.

But it was not long before I discovered the real purpose of the meeting. It had been organized by a man named Sleeper, who was a salesman for the Cody Trading Company. His customers were largely sheepmen, and he wished to curry favor with them. He arose and said he had punched cattle with Teddy. (I have seldom met a cowboy who has not punched cattle with Teddy!) He described his ability to do away with the Reserve, if they would delegate him to Washington. For the moment I seemed to fall in with the plan, and was myself appointed on the committee to raise funds for this trader's journey. The meeting ended peacefully, and immediately afterwards I wrote a personal letter to the President describing matters pretty thoroughly, with the result that the trader had his little trip to Washington in vain. He did not see the President, and the Reserve continued to exist.

A meeting was shortly afterwards called in Cody for the purpose of attacking the Reserve. At the opening of the meeting, John Chapman, a prominent rancher and cattleman, rose and said, "I want you to understand, gentlemen, that Mr. Anderson is a friend of mine. Anyone who says anything against him will settle the matter personally with me." His words were respected and nothing much came of that meeting.

But the enmity of the sheepmen did not stop there. Other incidents occurred from time to time which proved it to be far from dormant.

The following spring, while I was East, I had a letter from Mr. John Chapman in which he wrote: "I personally advise you not to return to Wyoming this spring, because if you do the sheepmen will kill you." In a postscript which amused me he added, "There is no use in sending you this letter. I know you will come anyway."

About this time I received the following letter about the Forest Reserve from Buffalo Bill Cody, who at that time was exhibiting his Wild West Show in England:

Olympia, London W.
March 26, 1903.

A. A. Anderson, Esq.
New York

MY DEAR SIR:

I am in receipt of your favor of March 14, and I here enclose you a copy of a letter I have just received from our beloved President Roosevelt. As the entire management of the Reserve is now placed in your hands, it will cause me no worry, and whenever I can assist you in any manner do not hesitate to call on me. In a few days I expect to own the Cody *Enterprise* [the principal newspaper of that section] entirely. Then that publication will be an out and out Republican paper, and it won't be published for the benefit of "Mr. Sheepherder." I am going to devote some space in the paper to patting the man behind the plough on the back a little.

I wish you were coming over here this summer, but much as I would enjoy a visit from you here, I will feel a little safer that you are out there in the Rockies, guarding not only our own interests but those of future generations. When you get to Cody, call on Mr. Ridgeley, my foreman, who will have a saddle horse for you that I take great pleasure in presenting to you. I only wish that I could spend the summer with you in the mountains but I am quite certain that my affairs are so shaping themselves that this will be my last season in the show business.

I hope you will write me occasionally from Big Horn County, and when you are sitting under the shade of a tree out there enjoying your pipe think of

Yours truly,
W. R. CODY

That same year a fire was started by the sheepmen at the head of a densely wooded canyon south of my property, with a sixty-mile-an-hour wind driving down the canyon towards my ranch. It was very dry at the time, and if the wind had not suddenly changed its direction, my buildings would have been lost. Not long afterwards I was awakened one night to find the ranch house actually on fire, without apparent cause. I had just fallen asleep when I was awakened by the tramp of a horse. I looked up and saw a man on horseback riding past my window and on around to the front of the house. I did not know but that the sheep-herders were going to carry out their threat and, as I did not intend to be trapped in the house, I took my gun and went to the front door. The man there told he had started for the ranch to see me on a business matter, but had lost his way, thus accounting for his late arrival. I took him over to the bunk house and had the foreman furnish him with a bed.

I returned to the house and was soon sound asleep. I was aroused at midnight by a violent knocking on my door, and heard Lieutenant Boyd, one of my rangers and the only other occupant of the house, calling to me, "Get up! The house is on fire!"

That day I had changed my bed, which formerly stood out in the room, and placed one side of it against the wall. Of course, on my first awakening, I tried to climb through the wall, but finally got to the living-room door and looked into a mass of flames and smoke. The kitchen was but a short distance away, and I succeeded in reaching it through the intense smoke and heat.

It was very fortunate that I could make my escape in this manner, as there were stationary iron bars in all the windows, which would have prevented my escaping that way. I was soon outside the house, but in my bare feet and night clothes, and there was snow on the ground. I went a short distance to my foreman's house, calling him to get up. Rush said, "What's the matter?"

"The house is afire!" I yelled.

"Is it bad?" asked Rush.

"You get up and see."

I went into his room and put on some of his clothes, borrowing a pair of boots, and returned to the house, which by that time was fairly blazing. Fortunately, I had put in waterworks, so I was able to attach a rubber hose and throw a stream of water over the house. There was also a pool near by from which buckets of water could be dipped.

At that time my house was the headquarters of my cow outfit, and I had quite a number of cowboys around, as well as some rangers. We organized a fire brigade and managed to extinguish the fire after it had burned only the center room; but that room was burned from floor to roof, and with it a fine collection of Indian relics and hunting trophies.

There were occasions when definite emergencies arose within the Reserve which called for quick and decisive action. One of these, I remember, came up when I was engaged on a tour of inspection in the Teton division. A telegram from Washington informed me that sixty thousand sheep had been put into that division without a permit, and asked me to investigate the matter and report. The supervisor of the division, Miller, verified the report. He declared he had not sufficient authority to prevent this trespass. The sheep belonged to four large owners in Utah, and were herded by forty armed men.

Thanks to our communication facilities and organization, I was now in a position to issue orders to rangers in various portions of the Reserve. I told them to meet me the following week at a place called Horse Creek, near Jackson Lake. About sixty-five of them came, in full regalia, armed and well mounted. Erect and clean, they made a fine body of uniformed men, and I was proud of them.

I ordered them to fall in and had them draw up in a line in front of me. I then told them in a few words what

I intended to do. I proposed to remove the men and their flocks from the Reserve and to use whatever force might be necessary. I had no authority to order the rangers to participate in this action and I did not wish any man to go unless he felt willing and was prepared to carry out orders. I then said I wished every man who was willing to do this to take one step forward. I was pleased to see that every man did so, and expressed my pleasure to the lieutenant, who was standing near me. In his hearty Western manner, he replied: "Superintendent, there isn't a man here that wouldn't follow you plumb to Hell!"

We marched during the day, making camp at evening not far from where the first band of sheepherders were herding their flock. I wanted to reach the sheep in good time the next day; so I told my orderly to notify the rangers that we would break camp the next morning at three o'clock. The tents of the rangers were pitched in a circle with a small camp fire in front of each, and my orderly went to each in turn. When he came to the tent next to mine, I heard a young German who was occupying it say, "If dat's so, den I go right quick mit myself to bed in!"

We started as planned the next morning. The first bunch of sheep we encountered were guarded by herdsmen who were having lunch in an opening under the trees. The sheep, some fifteen hundred in number, were grazing on the mountainside near by. I rode up to the herders and asked if they had a permit to graze sheep.

"We don't need a permit," one of them replied insolently.

They further refused to comply with my order to drive the sheep in the direction I indicated, saying that they could not drive sheep in the middle of the day.

"Put these men under arrest," I said to Lieutenant Boyd.

"We will show them whether sheep can be driven in the middle of the day!"

I had provided for such an emergency by having a sheepherder and his two dogs along; so we went up the side of the mountain, where a flock of fifteen hundred sheep were grazing. I ordered the sheepman with his dogs to cut out three hundred of the sheep as a lead bunch, which we started down the mountain slope. I then placed my rangers in single file on either side of the remaining sheep to keep them from "milling up," and started to drive them at full gallop down the side of the mountain.

When we arrived at the sheep camp I said to the herders, "You see we can drive sheep even at this time of day, and now I want you to drive these sheep as directed or I will drive them to the easterly border of the Reserve and turn them loose."

They saw that I meant business. Knowing that unless they took charge of the sheep, they would lose them for the owners, they decided to follow my instructions.

In the same way we gathered up four bands of sheep, owned by the four different owners that had sheep on the Reserve, and drove them all to the easterly boundary. We held them there, while I sent for the United States Commissioner at Cheyenne to bring an injunction restraining them from returning across the Reserve.

It took nearly a week for Commissioner Clark to arrive with the injunctions which were to be served upon the several owners. My first move was to serve an injunction upon the owners of the most southerly band, two brothers by the name of Jacobs. One of the brothers had gone to Salt Lake City for provisions, but the other was still in camp and was served with an injunction. Leaving two rangers near him and his sheep in a camp across the river, I hurried north to serve the injunction on the other owners.

After serving these injunctions, I knew the sheepmen were in a tight place. Their herds were on the eastern border line of the Reserve on the Green River, and could now neither advance nor retreat. Across the river from the Reserve they were confronted with a real menace. Cattlemen had settled up the valley of the Green River, who would stop at nothing to prevent sheep being driven on their ranges. To return to their ranches in Utah, across the Reserve, would make them liable to the charge of being in contempt of the United States Court.

That their position was far from enviable was soon proved by actual events. A day or two later, one of the rangers who had been stationed near the Jacobs brothers rode hurriedly into my camp.

"An accident has happened to the sheep!" he excitedly announced. "One of the Jacobs brothers (the one who had been to Salt Lake) came to my camp this morning and said the blankety-blank cattlemen of Green River had come up and killed his brother and eight hundred of their sheep, and furthermore had burned up their entire camp outfit without leaving even a sour dough pot!"

I asked the ranger what had been done about it. He told me that they had ridden over to the scene of the outrage. Here it was found to be true that eight hundred of the sheep had been killed, and the camp had been burned.

"But was the brother killed?" I asked.

"Well, he sure could swear all right!"

As a matter of fact, he had been struck over the head with a rifle, but not seriously hurt. I saw what necessarily must happen. The Jacobs brothers would be forced to drive their remaining sheep back over the Reserve to Utah. So I told the rangers to let them proceed unmolested, while I served the injunction on the other owners and turned them loose. These men also drove their sheep homeward across the

Reserve, and in three days not a sheep was left within the boundaries. Eventually, all owners were summoned to appear before the court at Cheyenne and were fined for trespass. Thus the incident was closed, and, from that day to this, there has never been another sheep trespass upon the Reserve.

CHAPTER XII

THE YELLOWSTONE FOREST RESERVE
(Continued)

SINCE the Forest Reserve surrounds Yellowstone Park on all four sides, I frequently had to cross it in carrying out my duties as Superintendent of the Reserve. On these occasions Colonel John Pitcher always gave me a cavalry escort and aided me in every possible way. Colonel Pitcher, Superintendent of Yellowstone Park, and one of the most efficient superintendents the Park has ever had, was greatly interested in game protection, and coöperated with me harmoniously for that purpose.

The first white man to visit the region now known as Yellowstone Park was a member of the Lewis and Clark expedition to Oregon in 1806. On the return trip, this man, John Colter, asked permission to leave the company with one companion to trap beaver in that locality.

This permission was granted and the two men went up the Yellowstone River, amazed and astonished at the wonders and beauty they saw everywhere. While coming along the Yellowstone, however, they were suddenly attacked by the Blackfeet Indians, an exceedingly hostile tribe. They killed Colter's companion and took Colter a prisoner to their encampment.

Deciding to have some sport at Colter's expense, they tied him to a tree to be a target for their arrows. The chief interfered with this scheme, however, and instead ordered

Colter stripped naked. He was then given the advantage of a certain distance and ordered to run, with the tribe of warriors in pursuit.

But the chief did not know that Colter was an exceedingly fast runner and a man of remarkable wind and stamina. He easily outdistanced all but one Indian, turned on him finally, wrested his knife away, and killed him. Then Colter plunged into the river and hid behind some driftwood. There he remained until dark, when he swam downstream to a landing on the opposite bank.

For seven days he wandered through the forests, unclothed, eating roots, berries, and small animals that he could capture. Finally, he arrived at the trappers' fort he had left. When he described his remarkable experiences, his friends readily believed his account of the Indian adventure; but when he told of the wonders he had seen in the present Park, they called him a first-class liar. And for years this region was called Colter's Hell.

The first official expedition was sent to the Yellowstone in 1869. Another more important commission looked over the territory in 1870. The members of this commission were astonished by the beauty of the region, and curious as to its wonders. Upon their report and recommendation it was decided to create there a national park, thus preserving it for future generations, and a bill to this effect was introduced in Congress in 1872. It was immediately passed and signed by President Grant on March 2 of that year.

I was nearly drowned in the Yellowstone River one spring at the time of a high flood. I had decided to cross over the river, but my guide, Rush, objected.

"Better not cross here," he said. "The current will carry you beyond the landing."

I did not listen to his advice, but started in. My horse was soon beyond his depth and was forced to swim on. The swift current quickly carried us beyond the landing I was trying to reach. Below was a high, steep bank, which my frantic horse could not climb. Unable to force him upstream, I had no recourse but to allow the current to carry us down, with the hope of finding a possible landing below, the horse, all the while, pawing furiously at the steep bank. Perhaps it was the frenzied strength of my horse, or maybe only luck, but we did manage a landing finally. And when we climbed out of the river, I saw on the bank the body of a dead horse, whose owner, I later learned, was a cowboy who had been drowned in attempting to cross the river the day before.

One day when I was camped on the Teton division, a tall, lanky Mormon on a small, thin cayuse rode into camp. The Yellowstone Forest Reserve at that point joins the Star Valley of Idaho, a valley some sixty miles or more in length that is entirely settled by Mormons. The Mormons, by the way, are some of the best settlers in Wyoming. They are very industrious, and sober and intensive farmers. Their ranches are the best in the state. They take only a small acreage and cultivate it intensively. Each year they raise various kinds of products, and that year, the product that is in demand they sell, keeping the rest for their home consumption. They also have coöperative labor. One family will make cheese for the community, another butter; and in this way their work is greatly facilitated.

My discussion with this Mormon came round to Mormonism; and he said to me, "I don't see why the Gentiles are so down on Mormons."

"They are not," I said. "There is only one point of difference now, and that is polygamy."

"Polygamy?" he said. "There is no polygamy now. It keeps me jumping sideways like hell to take care of one wife!"

I felt sorry for the horse he was riding, and from the kindness of my heart, I offered to buy him. We finally struck a bargain, and I bought the horse for twenty-five dollars. I never made a better investment. Under kind treatment and with plenty of food that horse rapidly grew and filled out, developing one of the most perfect dispositions I have ever seen in a horse. He was my private saddle horse for many years, and never did a mean trick. I have had other horses in the West that did nothing but mean tricks. When they were not bucking, they would suddenly try to run under the limb of a tree and scrape you off, and were forever trying to leave you afoot.

I was out hunting antelope one day in the neighborhood of my ranch, and coming across a herd of these animals, I got off my horse, one that I had always treated with the greatest care and kindness. I dropped the reins on the ground and left him standing. As a usual thing in that country when you drop the reins of a saddle horse on the ground, he will remain stationary for any length of time. I proceeded after the antelope and succeeded in killing one. When I returned to my horse, I found that instead of standing still he had continued to walk on. He would run ahead for a short distance and then stop and graze. And when I again approached, he held his head on one side so that he would not step on the bridle rein, and amused himself with another run. This continued until I had walked many miles, and with each mile feeling increasingly in the mood to shoot that horse. Finally he came to a small swamp and allowed me to mount quietly, as though nothing had happened.

When I first took charge of the Jackson Hole country in the Forest Reserve, it was one of the worst places in the United States, filled as it was with rustlers, convicts, and desperadoes. I started in with the aid of my rangers to clean it up. I was informed of three desperadoes who had a camp near Jackson Lake and were killing elk merely for their tusks. I sent them a written order to leave the Reserve.

A week or so afterwards I was riding all alone in that part of the mountains ten miles from the nearest ranger when, unexpectedly, I came upon their camp. As they had seen me, there was nothing to do but put on a bold front, so I rode directly up to the three men, all of whom were armed.

"I sent you an order to leave the Reserve," I said. "How is it that I still find you here?"

Two of them merely glowered at me in a sullen way, but the other was very loquacious. "We haven't been able to find some of our stray horses and it has taken us some time to get our traps together."

"How long will you need to get ready?"

"We can do it in a few days."

"I will give you a week for this purpose," I said, "and unless you are off the Reserve by that time, I will have you arrested and turn you over to the soldiers at Snake River Station."

With this I pulled my horse around and rode away. It would not have surprised me to hear a rifle shot, but nothing happened. I returned safely to camp and felt I was playing in luck. Dame Fortune is a fickle mistress; one instant her lips are glued close to your mouth, in the next she bites you in the neck.

Gradually the feeling against the Reserve subsided, though opposition from the sheep interests continued fitfully. At that time these interests held the key to Wyoming politics. It was just before a presidential election and some Wyoming delegates in Washington warned President Roosevelt that unless I resigned my post as Superintendent of the Reserve, the Republican party in that state would be defeated.

I wrote President Roosevelt, asking him to send out someone in whom he had confidence to investigate and report to him the conditions as they existed. Accordingly, he sent Gifford Pinchot to investigate matters on the Reserve. I was camped on the Teton division of the Reserve when, one afternoon, Pinchot rode into my camp, accompanied by Frank Mondell, Republican leader of the House of Representatives, and Senator Borah. We had a pleasant dinner and were sitting smoking around the camp fire when Senator Borah facetiously remarked to his comrades: "Boys, we are wasting our time. Has anybody got a rope?"

After accompanying me on a tour of inspection, Gifford Pinchot reported to the President that the Yellowstone Reserve was one of the best organized, patrolled, and administered forest reserves in the country. It was indeed gratifying to receive a letter from President Roosevelt saying in part:

Mr. Anderson, I believe you have the right ideas in forestry matters. Go ahead and carry them out, knowing that you have the Department of the Interior and the President solidly back of you.

And yet it has been said that President Roosevelt played politics. He never played anything; he was simply "it," in his genuine, straightforward manner. One of my principal reasons for giving seven years of my time to forestry matters was that I felt I was aiding him in one of the objectives so dear to his heart; namely, the conservation of our national resources. To have known such a man and worked with him, even in the smallest way, in trying to carry out his high ideals, was inspiration indeed.

Where there is so much difference of opinion, violent strife and friction, as there was in connection with this question of the Forest Reserve, there is apt to be a short circuit and electric sparks. But that is all over today and everyone is satisfied that the Reserve was brought into existence.

CHAPTER XIII

THE YELLOWSTONE FOREST RESERVE
(Concluded)

I HAVE always cherished a love of wild life and nature, and for years before the creation of the Yellowstone Reserve I had been interested in game protection. Consequently, when the Reserve became an actuality, I was appointed Assistant State Game Warden of Wyoming, and had all my rangers made game wardens without pay. They, too, became deeply interested in protecting the wild life of the country, and for the first time the game laws of the state were thoroughly enforced.

At that time the Indian tribes were permitted by the Indian Department to leave their reservation and hunt on the Forest Reserve, a privilege which they were exercising in and out of season, so that a tremendous amount of game was being slaughtered. Obviously one of the first steps towards game protection would be to correct this misguided activity. A letter from me to the Indian Department at Washington brought an end to all permits granted to Indians to hunt on the Reserve. It was a necessary step, and the amount of valuable game it saved is hard to estimate.

Killing elk for their tusks furnished another problem of game preservation. Formerly, these tusks had only a nominal value, but when the Order of Elks adopted them as the emblem of the society, they began selling for twenty-five dollars or more a pair. Naturally, this proved an incentive for a general slaughter of elk. For instance, I remember that one day one of my rangers arrested a man named Rogers on a charge of killing game out of season. Twenty-five fresh elk tusks were found in his pockets, proof enough that he had been shooting bull elk merely for the sake of their tusks, leaving their carcasses to remain rotting on the ground. I took the man before the judge at Jackson, and he was fined twenty-five dollars.

As he came out, he said flippantly, "Well, I'll have to go kill some more elk to pay the fine."

It happened that about the time of this incident, the Order of Elks was holding its annual convention in Salt Lake City. I wrote a letter to the convention, stating that, owing to the high prices paid for elk tusks, the noble animal for which their society was named was rapidly becoming extinct. My letter was read at the convention, and its purport was appreciated. A resolution was then passed, abolishing elk tusks as the official emblem of the order.

All this time the conviction had been growing upon me that the only real way to protect game was to establish a properly guarded game refuge where shooting would be forbidden at all times of the year. Game laws alone seemed futile. Such laws had been enacted in every state of the Union; witness, for example, the law that still exists in the statute book of the state of New York, imposing a heavy fine for the killing of buffalo! Nor does a mere limitation of the bag help materially. To find out the number of animals killed, it would be necessary to have a warden to follow every hunter.

But where game refuges are established and no one is allowed at any time of year to carry arms therein or fire a shot, a few game wardens will suffice to patrol the country and the law can be strictly enforced. On these refuges the protected game is certain to increase immediately and wander to the surrounding country, as there are no fences surrounding the refuges. Yet the game will always have a sanctuary to return to in case of need.

It was for these reasons that I finally created a large number of such refuges on the Reserve. As long as these are properly guarded, big game will always be found in that part of the mountains. The result, so far, has been more than satisfactory; for there is now more large game in this portion of Wyoming than in any other part of the United States. Also the game refuges in the Reserve take on an added significance when it is realized that the game in Yellowstone Park, because of the high altitude and snow, must vacate the Park in winter and seek the lower regions of the surrounding forests, where they are now secure in the refuges that have been established.

At one time a few of my rangers and I came across a young man with a deer tied on a pack horse that he was leading. As it was out of season, I had him arrested. I took him before the judge, but he demanded a trial by jury, as was his right. For a trial in that part of Wyoming a jury of six men was then sufficient, as the state was but sparsely settled. We finally succeeded in finding six men, and the court was held in the judge's home in a log cabin in the mountains. The judge, after having leafed over the statute books of Wyoming, told the jury to hold up their right hands. He then proceeded to swear them in. But just as he had finished, he looked again in the statute book, and said; "By God, I swore the wrong swore. I will have to swore you over again."

He swore them over, and the trial commenced. We had no difficulty in presenting our case, as the young man was found with the goods on him. There was no rebuttal, and the judge made his charge. The jury deliberated for a few moments, and brought in the following verdict:

"He did it, but we won't find him guilty this time."

As antelope were becoming very scarce in Wyoming, we had a law passed forbidding the killing of antelope at any time of the year. The result had been an astonishing increase in numbers. I estimate that on one part of the Reserve, in the vicinity of my ranch, there are probably as many as one thousand antelope, a state of affairs which never could have existed without this special law. Yet even now I sometimes cannot help harking back to the good old days when this most beautiful animal of the plains roamed in such herds as to impede the cattlemen. I remember that in the Red Desert, south of the Reserve, after a round-up, the cattlemen were sometimes forced to wait for an hour or more while the antelope, which had been caught in the round-up, were sifted out from the cattle.

Well-guarded refuges will always be necessary if we are to preserve our wild life. It is astonishing how quickly birds and animals recognize the refuges where they are being protected. On my first trip to Jackson Lake—a beautiful body of water in the Reserve just south of the Park, extending sixteen miles along the Teton Range—I was amazed to see the surface of the water literally covered by thousands of aquatic birds. Flocks of flamingoes would rise like pink clouds from the water. A few years later, I sailed again from one end of the lake to the other and saw but two Sheldrake ducks! How often, judging by results, the guns of hunters had reverberated across that beautiful expanse of water during the comparatively short time since my former visit. I was so impressed by the desolation of the scene that I requested President Roosevelt to make Jackson Lake a bird refuge. With his usual understanding of the importance of conserving wild life, he complied, and a few years later, when I made another journey to the lake, I saw that the birds had returned. There were thousands of ducks of various species, as well as pelicans, flamingoes, and countless other varieties of waterfowl.

From the utilitarian viewpoint alone, the protection of game has proved of great financial value to Wyoming. It has resulted in hunters being attracted there, each of whom has been obliged to pay fifty dollars for a hunting license, besides purchasing camp outfits, buying horses, and engaging resident guides. Thus the game laws have contributed in a large measure to the prosperity of the state. Game protection has also been instrumental in drawing tourists, whose love of nature prompts them to see this wild life and photograph it.

The Yellowstone Forest Reserve was the first large forest reserve in the United States.* Surrounding Yellowstone Park on all four sides and occupying space in three states— Montana, Wyoming, and Idaho—it covers about 9500 square miles, an area twice as large as the state of Connecticut. Apart from its size, however, the Yellowstone Forest Reserve is significant in that it has provided the inspiration and basic plan for the development of all our national forest reserves. By its success, it has proved the great value of the reserve system to our country.

Civilization, with its attendant cities, pressure, and waste, is hurrying westward. It will not be long before our national parks and forests reserves will become the true playground of every real American who appreciates out-of-door life and the precious heritage of our wild and romantic natural background. It is a pleasure to look upon a spot in

---

* Since then all forested land owned by the government has been made into forest reserves and all are organized and administered in the same manner.

the world that is just the same as the Lord first made it, and where the face of nature has not yet been battered by the brutal hand of man. Soon every patch of wilderness that remains will be a true oasis. The Yellowstone Forest Reserve in particular, through its connection with the Park and because it is one of the most wonderful spots in the Rocky Mountains, may play a prominent part in our country's recreation.

CHAPTER XIV

THE SHOSHONE DAM

I HAVE quoted above a letter received from Buffalo Bill Cody when I was in the midst of my conflict with the sheepherders. Cody's name has become a household word in America on account of his connection with the Wild West Show. He flourished before Prohibition, but he found in the process of time that he would have to be somewhat abstemious if he was to continue successfully his feat of shooting at glass balls. He, therefore, stopped drinking entirely during the months when he was with his show on the road. But at the close of the season, with a few congenial companions, he would go on a hunting expedition in the Rockies and play a star engagement. One season, when returning from the annual hunt, Cody camped with his cronies on the Shoshone River near where the town of Cody now stands.

When they had done justice to a dinner *bien arrosée* and were feeling at peace with the world, one member of the party felt inspired to make a proposal:

"Let's found a town here and name it after Cody!"

The resolution was passed and George Beck was delegated to pick out the site for the new city. He mounted a horse and rode up on a high bluff overlooking the river. Here he threw down his hat on the ground and came back to camp, saying, "Gentlemen, the city of Cody is founded."

On this high, wind-swept bench the town of Cody now stands. The man whose name it bears became greatly interested in his namesake. He put up a large hotel and some other buildings, and persuaded the Burlington Railroad to build a branch extending from the main line to Cody. He acquired several ranches and a coal mine, and obtained from the government, under the Carey Act, the grant of a tract of land consisting of many townships on the Shoshone River. Under the provisions of this Act of Congress the person receiving an allotment of land had to put water on a certain portion of it in a given time.

The period of grace on Cody's allotment of land had nearly expired when one day he came to me, saying: "I have a big project I want you to become interested in. I will take my ranches, the property I own in Cody, my coal mine, and the land I hold under the Carey Segregation Act and will place them all in one company and will make you President of this company if you will help me with this irrigation business."

I told Cody I did not consider the project feasible. It would be impossible for him to irrigate land along the Shoshone River unless he built a large dam at the canyon, and before commencing the dam he would need to have $3,000,000 in his vest pocket.

Being then in the Interior Department, I told Colonel Cody that if he would go to Washington with me and would turn back to the government the Carey Segregation, I thought I had influence enough so that I could persuade the government to build a dam in the Shoshone Canyon. He consented. We went to Washington; he returned to the government his land segregation; and I succeeded in persuading the government to build the Shoshone Dam. The construction was started at once. At the time of its completion, this was the highest dam in the United States, damming up the Shoshone River, and forming an immense lake above it. When completed it had cost the government $5,000,000.

The result has been an entire change in the valley below it. Formerly the valley was but an arid desert, covered with sagebrush and bunch grass. That plain today supports thousands of prosperous ranches with their swelling seas of miles upon miles of wheat, corn, and alfalfa. There are several towns along the railroad and hundreds upon hundreds of happy homes. The desert has been made to blossom as a rose. It is said that a man who causes two blades of grass to grow where only one grew before has not lived in vain.

PART
THREE

CHAPTER XV

MY STUDIO IN NEW YORK

IT must not be supposed that, in all this period during which I was occupying myself with public affairs in Wyoming, my interest in painting or my activity as an artist had slackened. The Wyoming interlude has, in fact, furnished subject matter for a number of important paintings, concerning one of which, "The Vanished Tribe," painted from studies made on the Crow reservation, I shall give some details in a subsequent chapter.

Paris had been my home for ten years. On account of the many advantages for art work there, I had been thinking of making that city my permanent residence, but I realized that a foreigner never becomes a native of France. A Frenchman can live in America for a few years, become naturalized, and be accepted as an American; but an American can live in Paris for twenty years and will find himself an outsider and patronized as an *étranger*. Having given considerable thought to the matter, I realized that if I remained longer in France my niche in America would be overgrown and I would be a man without a country. I, therefore, closed my studio in Paris and returned to New York.

In New York, however, I did not find a studio that suited me. Thinking other artists returning to America would be in the same situation, I decided to erect a studio building. I bought four lots at the corner of Fortieth Street and Sixth

Avenue, the former site of the Hotel Royal that had a short time since been destroyed by fire, and designed, planned, and erected the Beaux Arts Studio Building there.

My business friends said it was a foolish thing to erect so expensive a studio building in what was then the "tenderloin district." But I wanted the best, since it is usually the best or the poorest that pays. It is either one of the best apartments or a tenement house that makes the best profits. A man wants a Rolls-Royce or a Ford; one appeals to his pride, the other to his pocketbook, while the distribution of the intermediate products depends largely on salesmanship.

The top floor of this building I arranged for my own studio. Enough has been said of my travels in an earlier chapter to suggest to the reader the various sources from which I derived inspiration and accessories for the decoration of the Beaux Arts Studio Building and of my own studio.

One of the corners of the studio has an alcove that is Oriental in its fittings. It contains a window that I brought from Cairo. This was given me by Garnia, who was an architect for the Khedive; it came out of the old palace that he was at that time renovating. Garnia's brother was the architect who designed the opera house in Paris which had been completed and opened shortly before I took up my residence in the French capital.

While in Cairo, I become well acquainted with Paul Baudry, who decorated the Paris Opera House. I found him a most agreeable companion. He was going from Cairo to Athens and invited me to accompany him. I accepted his invitation and made arrangements to go, as I had long been anxious to see Athens. Just before our intended departure, I was sailing a steam launch on the Nile, and was overtaken by a severe khamsin wind, that bore on its wings clouds of sand from the desert. My eyes and mouth

SIXTEENTH CENTURY DOORWAY IN STUDIO FROM CHURCH IN VENICE

were filled with sand, but as I was sailing the boat, I was obliged to keep my eyes open until I reached the shore. This caused such severe irritation that I had serious trouble with my eyes, and the doctor kept me in a darkened room for a week. Baudry could not wait, and left for Greece without me. To have visited this shrine of art with so agreeable a companion and so great an artist as Paul Baudry would have been most delightful, and I was greatly disappointed that I was prevented from seeing the wonders of Greek art still remaining.

At the entrance to the studio is a large doorway of columns of hand-carved wood, which came out of a church in Venice. It was made in the sixteenth century and still has its original gilding.

When I commenced this chapter I had intended writing a description of my studio, but on second thought, I will give another writer's opinion and insert an article recently published in one of our prominent New York journals. The reader is fortunate in the parts I have left out.

In Fortieth Street, just off Sixth Avenue, there is the strangest and most bizarre sanctum that the heart of an artist could desire. The master of this sanctum is Colonel A. A. Anderson, and his studio apartment, occupying the entire top floor of the Beaux Arts Building, is the repository for innumerable rare and exquisite *objets d'art.*

The Colonel is a gentleman of courtly and gracious manner, of medium height with the erect bearing of a soldier, whose eyes light enthusiastically as he talks of his beloved art, and his vast workshop is a realm of delight.

In his studio are many beautiful portraits and landscapes, but more striking, perhaps, is a huge study in three scenes depicting an allegorical study in the life of Christ.

"One of the distinctions between man and animals," he explained, "is man's art. And true art must be founded on truth. I feel that the artist's mission in life is a high one; it is to make the world a more beautiful place to live in. The impressionists have tried so hard for originality, that they have drifted away from the old acknowledged tenets of art, as laid down through the ages by the masters, and instead of being original, they have succeeded merely in being eccentric, because their art is not founded on truth."

Also among the paintings in Colonel Anderson's studio is a beautiful landscape of rolling green hills and blue sky, tufted with downy bits of cloud, and in the foreground a log house guarded by stately trees. This is the Colonel's ranch in Wyoming where he spends his summers.

Then high on the wall is a portrait of a lovely Japanese girl; while occupying an easel in another part of the studio is a picture of the interior of Saint Pères at Chartres. The artist has caught all the awe and majesty of the old church; worshipers kneel at their devotions, and high above the altar the light filters softly through many-colored windows.

Besides the Colonel's engrossing love for his painting he has many hobbies. "I feel," he told me, "that everyone can better do the work to which he has set himself, if he is interested in a number of other things as well," and he has proceeded to live up to this belief.

For many years he has been an ardent huntsman, and his immense ranch in Wyoming, not far from the Yellowstone Park, offers limitless possibilities. He has also hunted extensively in Canada and Alaska. Over one of the doorways in his studio there is a huge elk's head with spreading antlers, and beneath it the blunt black head of a buffalo. And he has killed thirty-nine grizzly bears, besides, browns, blacks, and Alaskan bear. Incidently, the Colonel is president of the Hunters' Fraternity of America.

The studio itself is a gigantic room probably a hundred feet long and almost as wide. A great dome arches in the middle of the ceiling, and windows in the roof admit the light which is so essential to the Colonel's painting. As one enters the suite there is a cozy little reception room done in rose and gold, and through a mammoth doorway of fluted columns and cornices, taken intact from a sixteenth century church in Venice, there opens to one's delighted gaze the vast studio itself, with its many easels supporting pictures, some finished, some in various stages of completion. At the distant end of the room is a pipe organ on which the Colonel plays, as a relaxation from the strain of his work. Out of sight behind some concealing curtains is a mysterious little alcove done in Oriental fashion, where one may sit among the soft cushions. Stretched half across one of the walls is a Gobelin tapestry, and flanking it are two enormous medieval lanterns designed by Colonel Anderson.

Leading from the studio to a large balcony room is a wide, winding stairway guarded by a writhing, twisting dragon, from whose horrible mouth gushes, not sparks of fire, but water, into a clear little pool, fern-banked, and half hidden under the stairs.

Among the treasures in this balcony room is a great wooden chest of strange design, flanked by two armchairs done in gilt and saffron brocade, which had been the throne chairs of the great Mohammed of Tunis. In a corner reposes a huge ugly Buddha, some eight hundred years old, who gazes inscrutably, great fat hands folded on his rotund stomach. In another corner, sharing the dragon's vigil, stands an ancient suit of armor, which one almost expects to hear clank.

Another short flight of stairs leads to the Colonel's living apartments. The dressing room with its thick soft carpet, beautiful furniture, and silver toilet appointments are all of his designing. Over the dressing table are two lights, also his handiwork, which resemble the waxen, half-opened petals of the magnolia, and which shed a soothing rosy glow.

The bathroom, quite the strangest and most alluring imaginable, gives one the feeling of being at the bottom of the cool green ocean. The walls are of iridescent sea-green tiles, and a line of carefully matched abalone shells marches around the room. The washbowl is a monstrous seashell, scalloped edges and all, while the tub is a sunken pool over which is poised a scarlet sea anemone, which, to the uninitiated eye, resembles an inverted chrysanthemum of unusual proportions. This creature of the sea, by clever artisanship, has become a light, while from its tentacles gushes a shower bath.

And last of all, to soothe the most pernicious case of insomnia to slumber, there is the Colonel's bedroom. There, if anywhere, one could dream dreams. The room is mysteriously dusky, being lighted by four lights carved of Italian alabaster and resembling Grecian urns, set in niches in the four corners of the dream room. One turn of a switch makes them a soft cool blue, another turn and they are violet, and still another turn and they have become rose-colored. Like the rest of the apartment, practically the whole room, furniture, and appointments have been designed by the Colonel. But perhaps the crowning beauty of the room is the ornate fireplace made of rock crystal, brought all the way from an extinct geyser on his Wyoming ranch, and carefully fashioned to make the fireplace and mantel. Under the subdued lights the crystals glisten like a thousand diamonds, adding a touch to the fairyland.

The most impressive thing about all these rare curios is the fact that they do not follow any period in their arrangement or conception, having been culled from temples in the Far East, from obscure corners of the Old World, from everywhere, in fact, and arranged with a sweeping disregard for order; yet the effect is most artistic and pleasing. As Alice in Wonderland would have remarked, "Curioser and Curioser!"

CHAPTER XVI

INTERESTS AND ACTIVITIES IN THE EAST

THE author of the description just quoted reports me as saying that everyone can better do the work he has set himself if he is interested in a number of other things as well. My interest in public affairs has not been confined to Wyoming. John Purroy Mitchell, who was elected on a fusion ticket to the mayoralty of New York and is generally acknowledged to have given New York City one of the most honest business administrations that it has ever had, took lunch with me at my studio the day after his election. I congratulated him on his victory and said that, with his popularity and ability, he could become the next governor of New York.

He replied characteristically, "My ambition is to fill successfully my position as Mayor and I shall think only of that and not allow myself to be distracted by personal ambition."

In one of our conversations he told me he was very much exercised about the condition of the traffic in New York City and considered it almost hopeless, as, at that time, no traffic corps had been adequately organized. I told the Mayor that if he would appoint a traffic committee of the members whose names I would suggest, I would take the matter up and see what could be done. He decided to do so, and I had appointed on the committee prominent citizens and officers of various organizations that were more or less interested in traffic. Of this commission, Mayor Mitchell appointed me chairman.

During the period of the Mayor's administration I devoted almost my entire time to the subject. I was given rooms at police headquarters by Police Commissioner Arthur Woods, one of our best police commissioners. A traffic corps was organized, and five hundred mounted police; a corps of motorcyclists with an adequate number of patrolmen was recruited. For the first time were introduced oneway streets, the semaphores, and the red and green lights that are now universally used all over the country. The same organization has continued ever since, and I doubt if there is any city in the world where traffic is better handled than in New York City.

While Mitchell evidently gave New York City one of its best administrations, it looks as though New York did not wish to be well governed, because when he came before the city for reëlection he only received 150,000 votes from the citizens of New York.

Mitchell was exceedingly patriotic and had given considerable time to the study of military affairs; he had passed the examination at Plattsburg and had been made a lieutenant. Being desirous of helping the country, for we were then at war with Germany, he went to Washington hoping to get a commission in the army. He remained there a long time and made every effort to be appointed in the army and sent to France, but was prevented from obtaining a commission by the personal influence of President Wilson. Not that Wilson had anything against Mitchell; that the Mayor had been elected on a fusion ticket and in opposition to the Democratic party was his reason for preventing Mitchell from obtaining any position in the army. Major Squires, who at that time was head of the army aviation, offered him a position in the air squadron, and Mitchell decided to accept.

He returned to New York, and we had lunch together the day he started for California to enter the training school. I said to him, "Mitchell, you are a leader of men and I consider it exceedingly foolish to enter the flying corps and take part in single-handed conflicts in the air."

He replied, "Colonel, I have no idea of doing so, but it is only through the Flying Corps that I can be sent to France to serve my country. I shall go as a pilot, but when I reach the other side I will be transferred to some other arm of the service."

Poor Jack never got to the other side. He finished with great credit, received his license as a pilot, and was just about leaving for France when, sailing over Louisiana, he fell from his plane and was killed,—a great loss to his country.

Mayor Mitchell was asked to open the Universal Exhibition in San Francisco a number of years ago and, on the way out, he visited me at my ranch, where we made an expedition together in quest of a bear. But that is another story and will be told in a later chapter.

My personal encounters with President Roosevelt and with members of his administration were invariably such as to confirm my high estimate of him. With his robust health, his overflowing animal spirits, kind heart, sense of humor, his great mentality, and prodigious genius for friendship, Roosevelt got more out of life than many of his fellow men and gave a new zest to life to all who came in contact with him. I called upon him one day just after he had sent one of his scorching messages to Congress. The papers had taken considerable notice of it.

"Anderson," Roosevelt said, "the papers say they like what I said but do not like the way I said it. Now, do you suppose if I had sent a nice, sweet, ladylike letter to those numbskulls at the other end of Pennsylvania Avenue, they would have paid any attention to it?"

I was in his office at the time he was packing to leave, as Taft was about to take his place. He was tying up a bundle of papers, and said to me, "Big Bill will never get as much fun out of this job as I have. I've had a bully time." Roosevelt not only had a "bully time," but he made everybody happy about him.

One day, my brother-in-law, returning from a visit to the White House, told me that the President had said, "Dr. Blanchard, your brother-in-law, Anderson, combines the artistic and the practical more than any other man I know. These are the kind of men we need in this country." It pleased me to receive a word of commendation from one whose opinion I esteemed so highly as that of President Roosevelt.

Roosevelt was truly one of our most popular Presidents, and had it in his hands, before leaving the White House, to name his successor. He had long debated which of two men to name. Events that have since transpired indicate how mistaken he was when his choice fell on William Howard Taft rather than on Elihu Root. Mr. Taft was fitted preëminently, both by training and predisposition, not for the presidency, but for judicial work, as his rich years as Chief Justice indicate.

I was dining with Secretary Root the day that Roosevelt announced his final decision. Root's disappointment was apparent. He had given up an enormously remunerative legal practice in New York and had accepted a cabinet position as a stepping-stone to a further preferment. But the President was doubtful of Root's election because he had been a legal adviser to many important trusts. Perhaps he remembered what was said at the Gridiron Club: "Taft and the world Tafts with you; Root and you Root alone!"

What a different world we might today be living in had Root been named by Roosevelt instead! After President Taft's inauguration, Roosevelt purposely left on his trip to Africa, and designedly withdrew himself from political affairs in order not to interfere with the Taft administration. Taft had made certain promises to Roosevelt, especially as to carrying out Roosevelt's progressive ideas, but Taft was easily influenced by his surrounding, and soon fell into the hands of Joe Cannon and other reactionaries. Many of Roosevelt's pet schemes fell to the ground, a misunderstanding resulted between the two men, and the Republican party split, so that in the following presidential campaign Republican votes were divided. Thus Wilson was placed in the presidential chair by a minority vote. Had Roosevelt or some other red-blooded person been our War President, America would probably have entered the war when the *Lusitania* went down, carrying so many Americans to death. Then the Allies would have been victorious years earlier, saving the destruction of millions in lives and property.

When the Revolution occurred in Russia, the Japanese Government were anxious to know the attitude of the United States, and sent one of their prominent generals to ascertain our views. The day after his interview with President Wilson, this general spent the evening with me in my studio and freely spoke of the matter. He told me that Wilson was decided in his opposition. As we had at that time an army of ten thousand soldiers, under the command of General Graves, in Russia, Japan did not think it wise to interfere against our wishes. Had Wilson agreed to help put down the rebellion, the Russian Government would not have been overthrown, Bolshevism would not have been born, and today the inhabitants would not be eating brown bread wet with tears.

CHAPTER XVII

DINNERS AT MY STUDIO

In 1920 I invited some forty of my hunting friends to my studio, where we organized the Campfire Club of America. I was elected President and held that position for four years. At the end of this time, when I resigned as President, the membership had increased to two hundred and fifty and we had nine thousand dollars in the treasury. On this occasion the Club kindly presented me with a handsome silver loving cup some eighteen inches in height with the inscription: "Presented to A. A. Anderson in recognition of what he has accomplished in forest and game preservation."

Shortly after my resignation I was elected President of the Hunters' Fraternity of America, an organization interested primarily in forest and game protection. To qualify as a member of the Hunters' Fraternity one was required to have killed at least one head of big game.

The Fraternity gave a number of interesting dinners in my studio, where we were pleased to entertain some distinguished guests. One of the first of these occasions was in honor of Peary and Amundsen, on their visit to New York after having discovered the North and the South Poles. They met for the first time at this dinner. I had taken great pains to decorate my studio appropriately for the event. Near the ceiling were small electric lights arranged to look like stars; over that end of the room where Admiral Peary was to sit, were the Dipper and the North

Star; while at the end of the room over Amundsen's seat was the Southern Cross. White table covers, slightly starched and crumpled irregularly to look like snow, covered the table, while here and there were placed pieces of mirror that realistically suggested pools of water amid the snow. This illusion was strengthened by placing in the center of the table a model of an iceberg cut out of a huge block of ice seven feet high. From underneath the cake of ice a group of blue lights cast a cold, arctic light. About the base of the iceberg was absorbent cotton resembling snow, and wandering near by were miniature polar bears and seals.

When the guests entered, the room was dark except for the stars and the iceberg. The impressiveness of the decorations seemed to affect Amundsen particularly; Ellsworth told me that at the time they were crossing the North Pole, Amundsen was describing this dinner to him. Both Amundsen and Peary made excellent addresses.

When, as toastmaster, I introduced Admiral Peary, I spoke of his wonderful exploits in the Arctic region, of what he had done for science, and how for the first time he had discovered the North Pole. I also said that Captain Cook had claimed he had discovered the North Pole, but from the odor of his reputation I thought the pole he had discovered was a polecat.

In the course of his address, Admiral Peary made an interesting prophecy. "In the near future," he said, "the crystal air above both poles will be stirred by whirring plane propellers, and when that time comes, the inner polar regions will quickly yield their last secrets."

The Association was greatly stirred by these remarks, and we immediately formed a committee for the object of polar exploration by airplane. The result of these explorations is well known.

When Dr. Eckener arrived in New York at the time of

his first crossing in the Graf Zeppelin, I gave him a dinner at the studio. Amundsen was in New York at the time and was desirous of purchasing a Zeppelin to be used in a flight to the Pole. I, therefore, invited him to attend this dinner and gave him a seat next to Dr. Eckener. Dr. Eckener treated him very rudely, refusing to speak to him because, although his native land, Norway, had remained neutral, he had fought on the side of the Allies against Germany in the recent war.

Accordingly, Amundsen went to Italy, procured a dirigible there, and engaged Nobile as pilot. Nobile proved to be an unfortunate choice. Amundsen told me that before their flight Nobile had said that, on account of the weight, no unnecessary personal baggage should be brought along. Consequently, when they were ready to start, Amundsen had only the clothes on his back. But Nobile brought aboard the dirigible two beautiful new uniforms, several boxes of oranges, and other unnecessary things for his personal use. Nobile was so disliked that at one time the crew threatened to throw him overboard.

After Admiral Byrd returned from his flight across the North Pole, I gave him a dinner at the studio, at which dinner many of the most prominent explorers were present, among them Captain Bartlett, Ellsworth, Amundsen, and others. Nobile was also in the city, but Amundsen told me that if Nobile was present, he would not come. Notwithstanding his dislike for Nobile, when Nobile met with his accident in the polar flight, Amundsen started off in a plane in that tragic effort to rescue him and was never seen again. The Bible states: "Greater love hath no man than this, that he lay down his life for a friend," but Amundsen laid down his life for one who was not even a friend.

Amundsen was a saga, a Viking of the north, worthy of the highest admiration. At one time when I was in Alaska,

I saw a small vessel passing near the coast of the Bering Sea. I was told that it was the vessel in which Amundsen had just found the Northwest Passage from the Atlantic to the Pacific. This, to my mind, is one of the greatest discoveries that has ever been made in the polar regions. But at the time scarcely anything was said about the event.

CHAPTER XVIII

ADVENTURES IN THE AIR

I HAVE always been interested in aviation. I was one of the charter members of the Aëro Club of America, the first aviation club started in this country. When the airplane was finally perfected, I thought it would be desirable to have a central airport built. After thorough investigation I decided for the following reasons that Richmond, Va., furnished the best location. It has the best climatic conditions, being practically free from snow and fog, and having an average temperature of 58 degrees the year round. A large number of railway lines center there, and there is also deep-sea navigation on the James River to that point. I spent many days motoring about Richmond to find the best location for an airport. About four miles from the city limits, I found a desirable place called Seven Pines. The Battle of Seven Pines was fought there during the Civil War. Located on the Williamsburg and Charles City roads, it comprises thirteen hundred acres of ground and boasts of fifty thousand feet of highway, and railroad facilities. During the last war the property was owned and operated by the United States Government as an ordnance reserve, and was improved at an expense of over five million dollars. Eleven artesian wells, sewerage, and drainage systems were built, as well as a brick power house with a concrete stack one hundred and eighty-five feet high (ideal now for beacon lights). There was also an office building one hundred and four by fifty feet. Another factor in favor of this location was the topography. The thirteen hundred acres of ground were perfectly flat, easy to approach in every direction, and the surrounding country was sufficiently level to allow of emergency landings.

Everything considered, Seven Pines had all of the characteristics of the ideal airport. I successfully negotiated its purchase and began to build a landing field. Convinced, however, that it would be for the interest of the city of Richmond to have a municipal port, I offered to sell four hundred acres of land to the city for that purpose. The Richmond Chamber of Commerce was most enthusiastic and backed the project in every way. Other prominent citizens of Richmond also coöperated, particularly Mr. Robert A. Lancaster, Jr., the progressive secretary of the Westmoreland Club. Mr. A. H. Thierman, Governor Harry Byrd, and Mr. L. Calvin Miller also helped in many ways.

The Richmond Air Junction became a legal fact on November 27, 1926. But the city administration did not at first fall in with our views, and it was a long time before the Board of Aldermen passed a resolution to buy the land, although I had offered to sell it to them for less than cost. When the act was passed, they only appropriated the small sum of $30,000 with which to build the airport. Baltimore had just appropriated $2,000,000; Detroit the same amount; and Boston more. However, Richmond has its airport.

A short time afterwards I went to Texas and spent several months in flying a great portion of the state in the interests of aviation, and had the pleasure of helping to create interest in an airport for Laredo, a city of 35,000, and for other cities. I went to Laredo with my friend Major Hensley of the United States Army, who was in charge of the Kelly Flying Field of Texas. The Laredo Chamber of Commerce gave us a reception and dinner, and listened enthusiastically to our discussion of the importance of having an airport. We also met with the City Council the following day, where consideration was given to the practical problems involved. The Board of Aldermen then convened and passed a resolution appropriating $100,000 for building an airport. This airport has been of great benefit to Laredo, as it is now the port of entry and departure for mail and passenger planes flying between Mexico and the United States.

No one acquainted with the problem of flying heavier-than-air crafts can be unmindful of the hazards which still impede the progress of this means of navigation. The danger of flying in times of a low, dense fog is, so far, insurmountable. This danger was dramatically demonstrated to me during the time that I was a member of the committee on arrangements to make plans for Chamberlin's flight across the ocean. One day I left Richmond for New York with Chamberlin as pilot in the same plane in which he later made his flight across the ocean. When we left Richmond, the day was clear, but we had not proceeded far before a mist began to form along the Atlantic coast. When we reached Philadelphia, we dropped in on the landing field of the United States Navy to see some of the officers and remained to lunch with them. When we left Philadelphia the fog had considerably increased, but as we did not anticipate any great difficulty, we continued our flight. But we had not gone far before there was scarcely any visibility; so Chamberlin piloted the plane upwards some eight thousand feet to get above the clouds. A clear blue sky then opened above us, while below was a carpet of white, rolling billows. Thrilling indeed! You could overlook the clouds for eighty miles,—a magnificent view, but no place for a permanent residence, especially considering that I had not brought my harp with me!

MISS COLUMBIA, PAINTED ON CLARENCE CHAMBERLIN'S PLANE.
FIRST PAINTING TO GO TO EUROPE BY AIR

After flying above the clouds for a time, we had no idea as to our location; so Chamberlin volplaned down through the fog to get our bearings. Then the engine, chilled by the cold mists, commenced sputtering and missing, threatening to die completely. When we reached a sufficiently low level to make out objects, we found ourselves over the most densely populated part of Newark! A landing could not possibly be made at that place, but fortunately our engine, instead of stalling, picked up, and we turned back, making a forced landing at Metuchen. From there we took the train to New York.

Fog is the *bête noire* of the aviator. That day, in the same fog, two government pilots, starting from Mitchell for Langley Field, lost their lives in the ocean not far from that point. When flying in a fog over water, it is impossible to tell where the fog ends and water begins. Making a landing on water, moreover, is far more difficult than on land. Water is non-elastic. If you shoot a bullet at water, it will flatten out exactly the same as if it had struck a rock. When a plane flying at a high rate of speed strikes the water, it is literally torn to pieces, and only a wing or some smaller part of the plane may be discovered to tell of the tragedy.

On the outside of the Chamberlin plane I made a painting of "Miss Columbia." This was the first oil painting by an artist to go from America to Europe by air.

CHAPTER XIX

THE RICHMOND ART EXHIBIT

It was my honor to be invited by the Union League Club of New York to make an exhibit of paintings, the only one-man exhibit, I was told, that they had ever held in the Club. I sent a sufficient number of paintings to fill their gallery, among them a portrait of Dr. John A. Harris, which I had just completed, painted in his uniform as Commodore of the Columbia Yacht Club. There were a number of other portraits, figures, landscapes and still-life included. One picture in the exhibition showed a life-size nude woman reposing on a lion's skin and was called "The Lioness."

One day when I was in the gallery, I was accosted by an elderly gentleman who came to me and said, "Mr. Anderson, may I ask you a question?"

"Certainly," I replied.

"Will you please tell me what first induced you to paint a nude woman?" he asked.

"May I ask you a question?"

"Yes," he said.

"Will you please tell me what first induced God to make one?"

He then said, "But why did you paint her on a lion's skin?"

I replied, "Oh, I thought a bare skin and a lion's skin would make a good zoölogical contrast."

He asked no further questions.

THE LIONESS

The College of William and Mary built in the city of Richmond an art school and a large art gallery to which they very kindly gave my name, and, when it was completed, asked me to make the first art exhibition. I selected and borrowed from the owners fifty of my more important pictures for the exhibition.

This was very kindly received by the public. The following article taken from the Richmond *Times Despatch* describes the occasion:

The impression as one enters the exhibition of paintings by Colonel A. A. Anderson, distinguished New York and Paris artist, which opened today at the new Anderson Galleries of the School of Social Work and Public Health at Franklin and Shaefer Streets, is of light, color, action, a great variety of subject-matter and of various interests in life, extending over many years of active production.

The portrait of the artist's mother, "A Ma Mère," is seen at once as one enters the gallery. The expression of interest and faith in the work of her gifted son shines through a warm skin, beautiful and soft in its modeling. This is a fine noble piece of work.

The portrait of Thomas A. Edison on the opposite wall expresses deep thoughtfulness as he sits in a golden light, surrounded by his experiments, completed, and in process. These are represented in a truthful and scholarly way, but are kept secondary to the dominating personality.

The portrait of Mrs. Henry Adams Ashforth, which hangs beside that of Mr. Edison, is very brilliant in its red and gold and the fur, though brown, is full of delightful color.

The two interiors, "L'Église des Saints Pères, Chartres" and "Chartres Cathedral of France," are seen through gold light of glowing windows. The violet distance and the height of arches add to the sense of peace and beauty. The drawing is very fine indeed.

The portrait of the artist, Colonel Anderson, gives a vivid sense of his personality. This hangs at the right as you face the second room. On the opposite wall are landscapes and marines, very luminous, which have brilliant sunshine and clear sky, and clouds full of color.

The place of honor goes to "Vanished Tribe," an inspired work with its vision of the luminous beyond.

On either side are portraits of women differing widely, as should be the case in expressing such different personalities, one (the portrait of Mrs. N. W. Sloper) in silver and pink with silver tones, which extend into the still-life and background, the other (Mrs. Dreiser) in vivid light, which falls on red hair and gives great reality to the figure.

"Poppies in France" is a large canvas of brilliant beauty. The wheat field with its blossoms stretches into the distant hills. The young woman, in a hat which repeats the color of the flowers she holds against the shadow of a white dress, makes a picture which will delight everyone. This canvas created much comment when it was exhibited at the Paris Salon some years ago.

"The Spanish Dancer" is full of life and action, very fine in drawing and color. The cool light from above and the warm footlights give a fine contrast. This is a most spirited canvas.

"The Lioness" is a study of subtle gold and green, and warm flesh tones. The lion's head is a powerful contrast to the delicate beauty of the woman.

"Miss Betty Anderson" is an exquisite child, very well painted in her spring garden with its sunlight falling through the shadow of the tree under which she is seated.

"Taormina, Sicily," with its colorful houses and towering mountains in blue and violet against a sunlit sky, makes one long to walk down the stone path into the town beyond.

There are many studies of still-life which are painted with masterly ability. The coloring is rich, Oriental and flooded with light which delights the eye. The iridescent glass, the pottery of ancient peoples, the textiles of fine design and coloring and the arrangements are most beautiful.

Among the important and interesting canvases is a startling portrait of Judge Edward R. Finch, in his judicial robes.

During the exhibition I received many letters, among them one from Governor Pollard and also one from Henry H. Hibbs, Jr., Art Director of the College of William and Mary. Mr. Hibbs wrote:

We have had over sixteen hundred visitors the first week of the showing of your pictures. We have now started on the second week, and the attendance still continues good.

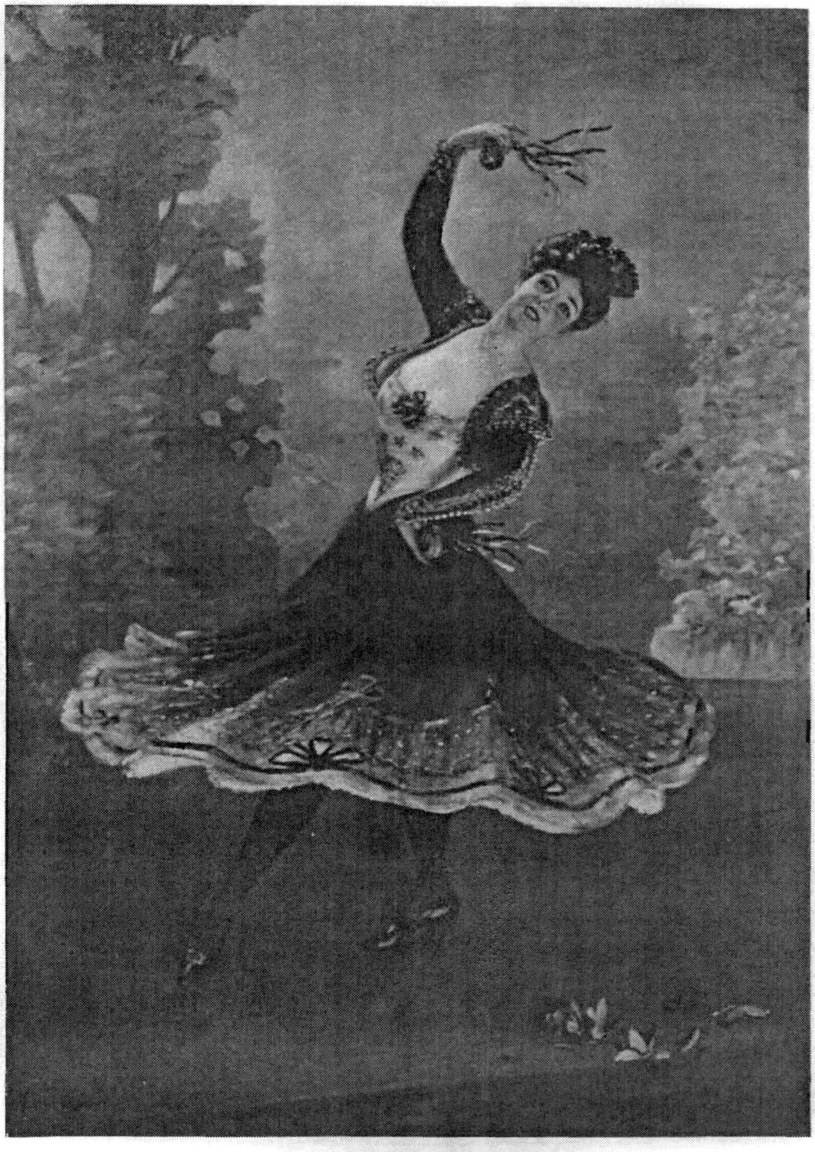

A SPANISH DANCER

We have had an unprecedented amount of favorable word of mouth publicity since the exhibition started. Nothing like it has happened here before in the field of art. I wish you could hear the comments. They are so gratifying.

The people here certainly like those pictures. Many return again and again. I have never heard anything that I have worked on, in the fifteen years I have been here, so highly praised and so universally pleasing to all. I know you have worked hard on this exhibition, and I want you to know that your efforts have counted. The people appreciate it.

If a man's true home is where he is loved and honored, and where his personal traits are admired, then you have a home in Richmond, for certainly your pictures have pleased many people, and your kindly, genial spirit and your unselfish work have won many hearts.

In the fifteen years I have been working here I have met no man so uniformly considerate and generous with both time and money and self; with such ready sympathy for what I have tried to accomplish. It has been a source of much satisfaction and personal joy to know you, and the conversations we have had and the work we have done together I will never forget. I will keep you informed as to what goes on from time to time. I hope you are enjoying yourself. All of us miss you and are looking forward with much pleasure to your return.

The Honorable John Pollard, Governor of Virginia, wrote:

DEAR COL. ANDERSON:

On yesterday afternoon I visited the A. A. Anderson Art Gallery here, and I am writing to tell you how deeply grateful I am for what you are doing to promote the appreciation of art in Richmond and in Virginia.

When you are next in the city, I should like very much to have the pleasure of a visit from you.

With best wishes, I am,

Cordially yours,
JOHN GARLAND POLLARD
Governor

Apparently no picture in the exhibition attracted more general attention than the portrait of my mother. At the opening reception a sweet-faced, gray-haired lady came up to me and said, "I have just been out and bought a dozen roses that I would like to place beneath your mother's portrait."

Nothing ever was said that touched my heart more. As I say in my dedication, no one man accomplishes anything worth doing in life without having his mother to thank for it. More than one man can take the place of a father to us. We can have many brothers and sisters, but a man has only one mother. And the word "mother," which is similar in so many languages, is the first word a baby learns to lisp and the sweetest of words. I had a wonderful mother, a mother who during her entire life had but one thought and that was her children. I once heard her remark, "I hear people say what a great trouble their children are to them, but when I get my little ones tucked into bed and kiss them good-night, I feel more than repaid for any trouble they have been during the day."

There is a peculiar thing about a mother's love. She loves each one of her children with her whole heart and yet loves them all equally. Mother had a bright mind, clever and witty. I wish I had written down some of her shrewd observations and witty sayings. I never kept a diary, however, and am writing entirely from memory. I recall one amusing remark she made during one of my visits to my family. I had returned from Paris, where I had become accustomed to the French habit of having breakfast in my room. The first night, as I was about to retire, I said to my mother, "I would like to have my coffee and roll in bed."

My mother replied, "You can have your roll in bed, but if you want your coffee you will have to come down stairs."

As I have said, my mother's entire life was devoted to

PORTRAIT OF THE AUTHOR'S MOTHER

her children. She lived until she was eighty-nine years of age. When her last moments came, my sister was sitting at her bedside. Mother, who was scarcely conscious, said, "Give me a piece of work." My sister handed her a handkerchief; my mother took it and went through the motions of sewing. She then folded it, laying it aside, and said, "Now I have finished something for one of my children," and passed away.

One of my important pictures at this exhibition was entitled "The Vanished Tribe," which I had painted the previous year from studies made on the Crow reservation. In the center of the picture is an Indian standing on a high point of rock looking across the valley into the sunset sky, and across this sky is a long procession of phantom Indians that he sees as visions of his buried tribe. I painted this Indian picture not only in the hopes of producing a work of art, but as propaganda for the Indian, whose mistreatment I have discussed in an earlier chapter.

I have composed the following lines about this picture:

THE VANISHED TRIBE

An Indian stood on a rocky crest
Watching the sun as it sank to rest,
His thoughts dwelt on the distant past
When the Indians owned that country vast;
Mountains and valleys and boundless plains
Throughout that land supreme they reigned,
Then the dark forests were filled with game
And millions of buffalo dotted the plain.
Along the streams their tepees lay,
Where little papooses were seen at play,
And in the forest and in the glen
Were dusky maidens and bravest of men.

As his eyes wandered on the distant haze,
A marvelous sight met his gaze—

Marching across the broad expanse
He saw a sight that thrilled his glance.
Dimly he saw at the decline of day
A host of Indians in martial array.
Far in the distance as the eagle's flight
They marched and marched in the dim twilight.
To him it seemed a tense, hard dream,
Its wondrous color and its brilliant gleam.

He saw as he stood on the mountain's crest
A vision of his tribe long gone to rest.
As they marched across the crimson sky,
Not a murmur was heard or battle cry
From the phantom host of buried braves
Now marshalled again beyond their graves;
As death had come and opened the door,
They now before him appeared once more.
Weary and worn they wended their way
To the "Happy Hunting Ground" ever to stay,
They had bravely lived and bravely died,
And he viewed them all in lofty pride.

Then out of the sky and across the plain,
There came to his ears this sad refrain—
    "In this land is a God we trust,
      A God we pray to be so just,
        That never again we must be thrust
          From our Happy Homes, by the white
            man's lust."
Afar in the distance he sees them ride,
As he stands alone, the last of his tribe.

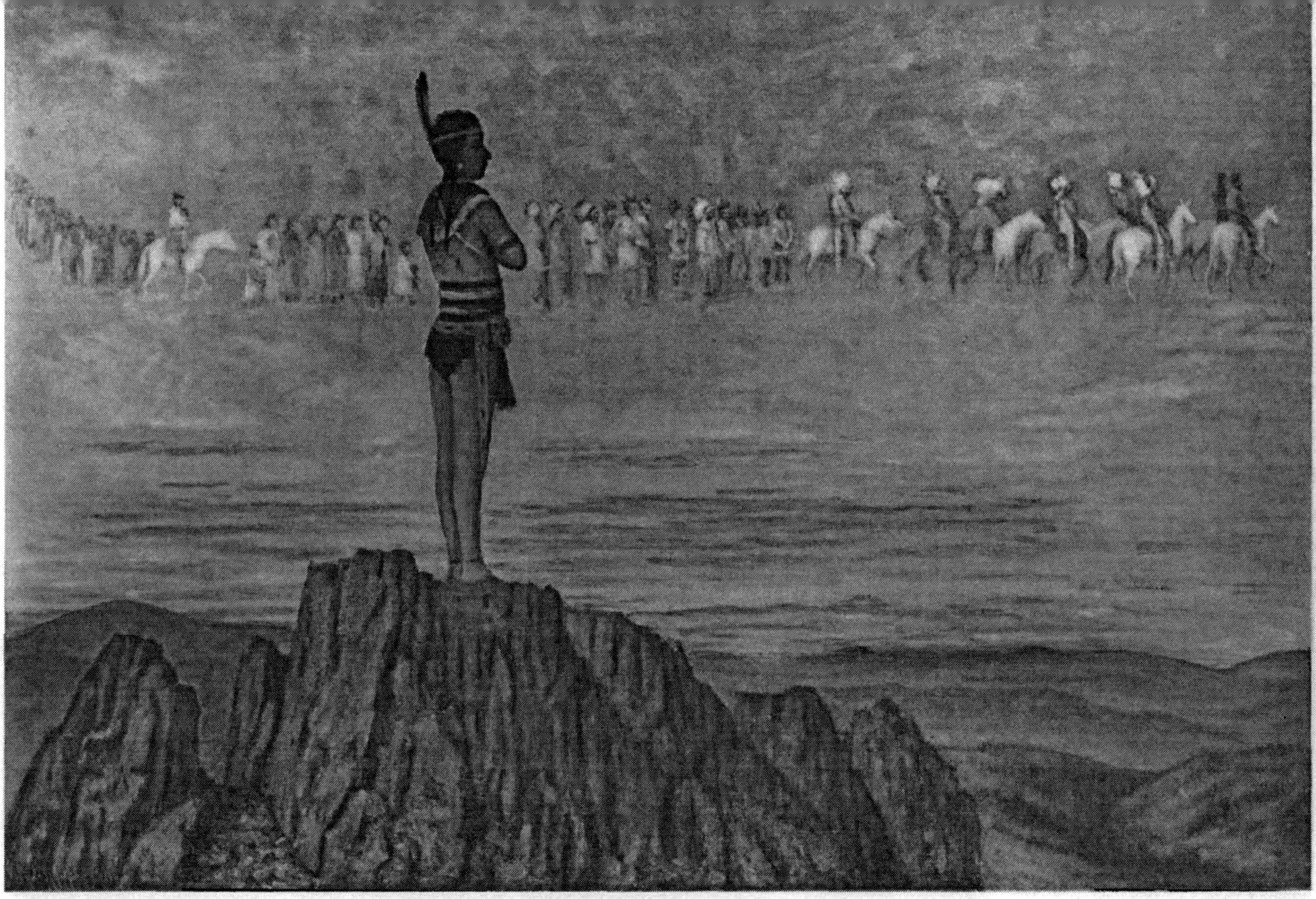

THE VANISHED TRIBE

PART
FOUR

CHAPTER XX

MY DOG FRIENDS

I HAVE always had a great affection for dogs. The dog was the first animal domesticated by man, though it is a question whether a man first adopted a dog or a dog a man. When America was first discovered, dogs were the only domesticated animals that the Indians had. At that time there was not a horse on the continent. This seems strange, as the earliest skeleton of the primitive, five-toed horse was found in Wyoming.

As a small boy, I was constantly picking up some lame or mangy cur on the street and bringing him home, much to my mother's annoyance, as she said it brought too much dirt into the house. But with tears and pleadings, I usually gained her consent, and the dog and I would become inseparable companions. One time, having saved a few pennies, I looked up a photographer and had a daguerreotype made of one of my friends, whose picture may be seen in the accompanying illustration.

During my life I have owned many dogs; at one time I had fifteen on my ranch. Prince Dolgoruki of Russia made me a present of two borzoi, or Russian wolfhounds, that came out of the Czar's pack at Moscow, and fine specimens they were. I was living in Paris at the time and exhibited them at the Paris Dog Show, where they took first prize. They were also exhibited at a bench show in New York City the following year and again received first prize. I took them to my ranch, where they presented me with a litter of six little wolfhounds which grew and flourished. When these were grown I had a pack of eight, all of them perfect beauties. I had expected to use them for hunting wolves and coyotes, which were numerous in that part of the mountains. They did not prove of any value for this kind of hunting, however, even though the borzoi is probably the only dog in the world capable of handling a wolf. They run entirely by sight, and not having keen scent, they would lose track of the wolf when he dropped behind a bank or a washout. While they could not follow a trail, they were exceedingly bright in many ways. I had considerable sport with them hunting jack rabbits. At the same time I owned a bird dog which would accompany the pack of wolfhounds. When he scented a jack rabbit concealed in the sagebrush, he would come to a point. The hounds, which had been watching his movements, would then rush in and pursue the frightened rabbit. Even though a jack rabbit can run exceedingly fast, he was never a match for these hounds. After running for some distance, a rabbit usually doubles back quickly, and one of the hounds which had been hanging back apparently waiting for this event, would then capture him.

I once owned the most intelligent dog I have ever seen. His name was Figaro, and I purchased him in Paris at the Jardin d'Acclimatation, where I found him in a large cage of caniches, or French poodles. He was exceedingly bright and attractive. I took him along with me to Les Andelys, where I was painting that summer. When I returned to Paris, Figaro accompanied me. I thought he would be delighted to see his old friends at the Jardin and, taking a cab, I drove to that place in the Bois de Boulogne. When I got out of the cab at the entrance to the Jardin, Figaro pulled back and refused to enter. I pulled on his leash, and

DAGUERREOTYPE OF AUTHOR
WITH HIS DOG

insisted on his following me. When we reached the front of the large cage where the other dogs were kept, he turned his head away and refused to look at them. He was very unhappy until I took him away, evidently afraid of being left there.

The next day I was lunching at a restaurant in the Palais Royale. I had ordered some mutton chops, which looked very attractive to Figaro, who was seated on a chair next to me. I gave him a piece of bread, and he immediately spat it out upon the floor. I had already taught Figaro to eat anything I gave him, and when I said, "Figaro, get down and eat that," he obeyed me, getting back again on the chair and renewing his interest in the chops. I gave him another piece of bread. He sat there and pretended to chew, then slumped down off the chair and went across the restaurant to the opposite side, and deposited behind a curtain the piece of bread I had given him. I rewarded his cleverness by giving him some meat.

When I returned to New York City I brought Figaro with me, and no dog ever made more friends for the canine race. Even my mother, who had not gotten over her dislike for dogs, became fond of Figaro. At first he was not allowed above the street floor of the house, but one day when I was in my room upstairs he started to come up. My mother, who was sitting in the library with the door open, saw him, and called him back. He immediately returned, lying down on the floor in the hall, and my mother continued reading. Presently she saw Figaro quietly looking around the corner of the door, and when he saw her absorbed in her book, he slipped by the door and quietly sneaked upstairs. My mother thought he was so clever that she did not recall him.

Figaro would play hide and seek with the children and enter into the sport with as much enthusiasm as a child. He would take his turn at hiding, and he was usually very clever in the spot he selected, going under a bed or in a dark corner. The children would whistle and call for all they were worth, but he would not pay the slightest attention until one of them actually found him. He would then come out and wag his tail happily. He would also take his turn at standing in a corner putting his paws over his eyes until he heard a childish voice say "Ready!" With his sense of smell, he could, of course, easily find them.

Figaro soon learned all the tricks that dogs know. He would walk on his hind legs as well as on all fours, would make believe dead, jump through a man's extended arms, and do many other clever and amusing tricks. He spent the daytime in the studio with me, and when a strange visitor entered, he would of his own accord start going through his various tricks, knowing that since he would probably have to do them anyway, he might as well get them over with. When an accustomed visitor entered, however, he paid no attention to him. A strap was attached to the latch of my front door, so that Figaro could pull it and open the door. When the bell rang, he would immediately answer it, and, opening the door, admit the visitor. If a card were offered him, he would take it in his mouth, and, walking on his hind legs, bring it to me.

I kept Figaro clipped, as French poodles usually are, with a mantle of fur about his shoulders, a moustache, and cuffs on his feet, but the rest of his body closely clipped. He was as proud of himself, when he had been freshly clipped, as a girl with a new dress. He would turn his back around to each person in the room to be admired. A caniche with his trimmed hair was an unusual sight in New York City at that time. He attracted considerable attention on the street, particularly from the newsboys and messenger boys, who would stop Figaro and examine him, much to his annoyance.

One day the doorbell rang; he went to the door to answer it, but returned to the studio alone. The bell rang again and again, and I told Figaro to go and open the door, but he would not move. I finally opened the door myself, and there stood a messenger boy, who said Figaro had opened the door, and then slammed it in his face.

If Figaro saw a cat on the street he would rush at her with the greatest fury. Should the cat run, he would bravely continue the pursuit, but should she stop, hunch up her back and show fight, Figaro, in the most nonchalant manner, would go around hunting for a bone as if he had never seen her.

One day Figaro accompanied me when I went to call on a lady friend. It was a rainy day and upon entering the house I left my rubbers and hat at the door, telling Figaro to lie down and wait for me. I went upstairs to the library and stayed there some time in conversation, when I heard Figaro coming up the stairs. I told him to go back. He returned but in a short time he came in again, carrying one of my rubbers in his mouth. This he laid at my feet. I took the hint and departed!

I could send Figaro upstairs to get my hat or cane or gloves and he would never make a mistake. Often, when riding horseback along a country road, I would intentionally drop a glove, and ride on for some distance; I would then tell him in an ordinary tone of voice that I had lost my glove. He would immediately take the back trail, find my glove, and come up standing on his hind legs and give it to me.

Figaro loved to make himself useful, a trait well illustrated when I was staying at my brother's house in New Jersey. When my sister-in-law, Mrs. Anderson, went to do her morning marketing, Figaro always went along and insisted on carrying her passbook. Returning one day, Mrs. Anderson neglected to ask Figaro for the book. Unable to

find it the next morning, she said, "Figaro, where's that
book?" He went out the front door and over to the adjoining garden of a neighbor, where he began digging in
a flower-bed. Mrs. Anderson called to him. He looked up,
but kept on digging until he finally unearthed the book and
brought it to her.

I had taught Figaro to retrieve. He was as delighted as
any bird dog at the sight of a gun, would follow me, and the
instant I shot a bird, would run and retrieve it, but there
came a change in his idea in the sport of hunting. At my
house in Greenwich I was one time trying out a new rifle
before taking it West. Figaro had accompanied me to the
field where, looking around for a mark to shoot at, I saw a
woodchuck sitting on a low stone fence. I shot at the
woodchuck and hit him. He fell over on the opposite side
of the stone wall, and Figaro rushed in to retrieve him.
When I reached the fence and looked over, I found the
woodchuck was trying to retrieve Figaro. They had a desperate fight, and Figaro showed great bravery in finally
killing the woodchuck. After that I never could persuade
Figaro to follow me when I had a gun. He absolutely
refused, saying, "If you get fun out of hunting, that's all
right, but my line is full."

Not feeling very well one day, I was lying on the lounge
in my studio alone. Figaro seemed to realize my condition
and appeared to be very anxious about me. A girl model
whom I was painting at the time came into the studio and
over to the lounge to shake hands with me. Figaro objected
to her attentions, however, growled, and grabbed her by
the wrist. From that time he took a great dislike to this
model, growling every time she came to the studio. Figaro
never injured anything in the studio except on one occasion.
I had painted a head of this model and just before going
to lunch one day placed it against the wall with the face

FIGARO

exposed. Figaro was left alone in the studio, and while I was gone he completely destroyed the picture with his claws.

Poor Figaro met a tragic end. While in Paris I had left him with my brother, where he was one of the most loved members of the family. One moonlight night, being a Frenchman, he took his guitar and went up the road to serenade a mademoiselle. Here he evidently met a rival who proved too much for him, for the next morning my brother found his dead body along the roadside.

In England I purchased two Bedlington terriers, of a breed little known in this country, although it is one of the best of the terrier family. I named them Pero and Dora, brought them to America, and took them to my ranch. Dora had a litter of pups, and even before their eyes were open these babies would fight until they were bloody. The Bedlington terrier is probably the most pugnacious of dogs.

One day while hunting, I encountered a large cinnamon bear. Pero and Dora immediately started in pursuit, overtook and attacked the bear. When he started to run they would snap at his heels. He would turn around and charge them, but the dogs, being exceedingly active, avoided him. They thus kept on annoying, until I came up. I was afraid to shoot, however, for fear of hitting one of the dogs. Just as I arrived at close quarters, the bear charged, grabbed Pero by the back, gave him a violent shake, and threw him about ten feet. I thought that was the end of Pero, but the bear had only caught him by the loose skin on his back. His teeth had torn a rent of ten inches there, but in spite of this, Pero immediately rushed up again and jumping for the bear, grabbed him by the ear. I shot and killed the bear, or the dog would certainly have been killed.

I lost Dora later from porcupine quills. The porcupines

are very numerous about my ranch and the dogs are constantly getting into trouble with them. It is a strange thing that, no matter how often a dog, attacking a porcupine, is severely hurt by the quills, he never seems to learn his lesson and will attack the next porcupine he meets. Dora attacked one too many, and when I found her she had quantities of quills sticking out of her in every direction. I spent some time with tweezers trying to extract them. A porcupine quill is barbed, so that when it strikes it will continue to bury itself in the flesh. When Dora died, I made a post-mortem and found that some of the quills had worked into her lungs.

One day a black and tan bitch came into the ranch house. Where she came from I had no idea, as my nearest neighbor was fifteen miles away. But wherever she did come from, I fear she had not been leading a moral life. One month after she had sought refuge at the ranch from the cold, cold world, she had a litter of pups. As an actual fact, one was a black Newfoundland, two were brown and white spotted pointers, and one of them a bulldog. Each of them was as distinctly marked as if it had been a thoroughbred. I think she herself felt somewhat ashamed of her deed, for after she had deposited her illegitimate family at the ranch she pulled out, never to show her face there again. Perhaps, with a look of innocence on her countenance, she had returned to her former home.

CHAPTER XXI

HUNTING BEAR IN THE ROCKIES

BEAR-HUNTING is interesting and exhilarating because it contains a slight element of danger. At one time I had a neighbor named Vedder who, in partnership with another man, owned a ranch a few miles below mine. One day his partner went to a near-by town to obtain provisions while Vedder remained at the cabin. Just before dark he happened to look out of the cabin and saw a grizzly bear coming down the mountainside. He went out with his rifle and shot at the bear, but failed to bring him down. The bear attacked him, tore out his left arm, and apparently left him for dead. The man came to, however, crawled back to the cabin, and wrote with a pencil on the fly-leaf of a book a short account of what happened. His last words were "My God, how I suffer!" His partner returned and found him dead.

While hunting near my ranch one time, an acquaintance of mine came across a bear. He shot at him but missed. The bear charged. The hunter dropped his rifle and climbed a near-by pine tree. The bear camped at the foot of the tree for some time waiting for him to come down. As this prospect was not inviting to the man, however, he remained in an uncomfortable position up the tree until finally the bear pulled out. After waiting some time longer to make sure that the coast was clear, the hunter descended, picked up his rifle, and started back to camp.

159

But the bear, instead of leaving the vicinity, was hiding in some bushes near by, and jumped out, and killed the man before he had a chance to shoot.

It was during one of my early camping trips with John Claflin that I had my first encounter with a bear. We had made an early camp and as we were out of meat I had decided to try my luck at getting some venison. I rode for several miles without sighting game and was on the point of turning back, for it was getting late, when I happened to look down a little valley covered with bushes. There in the distance was my game, three deer, I thought. I dismounted and approached them. Arriving at the spot, I looked across some bushes but saw, instead of deer, three bears standing on their hind legs feeding on wild raspberries. One of them was a very large bear, and the other two, half-grown cubs.

I took careful aim at the largest bear, and in rapid succession fired two shots. The bear fell, and I shot and wounded one of the cubs. The other cub disappeared behind some bushes and I did not get a shot at him. I walked round a patch of undergrowth and saw the large bear lying on the ground rolling from side to side, moaning. I thought her back had been broken. The small bear was lying on his back yelling for all he was worth; so I put a bullet through his neck to silence him. When I attempted to fire again at the big bear I found my gun empty!

I hunted through all my pockets but could not find a single cartridge, as I had brought only those in the magazine of the gun. The bear seemed unable to get up; so I took out a clasp knife with a three-and-a-half-inch blade that I had with me. I opened this knife and was tying it to a pole I had picked up. I am not sure what fool thing I was going to do with it. In fact, I didn't have a chance to find out. Before my nervous fingers could com-

plete their task, the bear got up on her hind legs and jumped
at me, apparently as good as new.

A most fortunate accident then occurred which, doubtless, saved my life. Standing by my side was my dog, a
Gordon setter, which had not taken the slightest interest in
the combat. In fact, he seemed partially dazed. When the
bear jumped, I jumped! I ran, the dog ran, and the bear
ran after us. Strangely enough and fortunately, the dog did
not stick to my heels but ran off to the right. The bear
luckily took after the dog; otherwise, she would have had
me in two jumps. I reached a higher elevation, turned back
and watched the pursuit. The bear, being wounded, could
not run as fast as the dog, and after chasing him about a
quarter of a mile, she turned around and returned to lie
down beside her dead cub.

I did not now propose attacking the bear with a knife, so
I found my way back to the horse and rode into camp to
relate my experience. Early the next morning we returned
to the spot where I had shot the bear. But she was nowhere
to be seen, although near the dead cub was a pool of blood
where she had lain. We started to follow her trail but it
led over dry shale, thus leaving no track that we could
follow. I never again saw that bear, the first grizzly I had
ever shot at. How true are the lines at the end of La
Fontaine's fable: *Il ne faut jamais vendre peau de l'ours
avant de l'avoir tué*.

The bear is an extremely interesting animal, and I have
given considerable study to his habits. A bear is very tiny
at birth, scarcely larger than a rat, but full-grown, he sometimes weighs as much as twelve hundred pounds. The contrast between the cub and the full-grown bear is almost
unbelievable. The baby, ten inches in length, grows to be
ten or twelve feet, and the Alaskan bear becomes the largest
carnivorous animal in the world.

When born, bears are blind, toothless, and almost hairless. For two weeks they are practically helpless. The mother keeps close within the den until the cubs are two months old. She does not leave them even to secure food or water, but lives as she has all winter on the layers of fat she accumulated before hibernating.

Perhaps it is also a mother's love that keeps her secluded. The male bear, a cannibalistic animal, leaves his winter home very hungry; he would find the young cub a very succulent morsel.

The bear hibernates for several months during the winter. While a bear remains very thin during the summer, in September he commences to put on fat. By late fall he will have acquired a layer of fat on his back four inches thick. He does not dig in the soft earth to make a cave, as naturalists have related, but wanders through the mountains and, when a particularly cool night comes, seeks shelter under an overhanging ledge of rock or finds a natural cave in the mountains, where the long sleep is begun. There the bear remains in a torpid condition until spring. He scarcely breathes, the blood merely circulating at a slow rate through his veins.

As I have said, the bear at the time of autumn is exceedingly fat. During the winter he subsists only on his fat and when the sun awakens him he leaves an absolutely clean cave; the bear will weigh as much then as at the time of hibernation, but the fatty tissue will have become factice. In less than a week after leaving his retreat, however, this factice will disappear, leaving him very lean and hungry. When a bear first comes out of his hibernaculum in the spring after a long period of fasting, he is exceedingly hungry and will spend almost the entire day roaming around in search of food. The food of the bear in the spring consists of grass, small sprouts on the bushes, roots that he digs up, and insects. I have seen a bear put his paw on a black ant's nest, soon to have it covered with infuriated ants. He then deliberately licks them off and repeats the operation.

The ant is the most intelligent of all insects. The ant hills that are built in Wyoming are made of pine needles, bits of sand, and other débris, a foot or more in height. I have often been able to find my direction by the convenient ant hills. I merely remove the top of the mound to find where the nest is prepared to receive the eggs. These are always deposited in the southeast corner, for at that point they will receive the warmth of the early morning sun.

Bears also eat grubs. I have seen a bear go along a mountainside and turn over every rock, from a small one, not larger than a man's hand, to extremely large ones. Underneath he finds white grubs which he proceeds to lick off. (Insects lay their eggs beneath a stone because the stone keeps the heat of the sun during a large portion of the night.)

Bears are also fond of berries and feast on them in season. During the late summer they subsist largely on a meat diet, killing calves of the elk. They are also fond of carrion, and later in the season resort to the killing of cattle. One season I thus lost on my ranch twenty-five head. The teeth of the bear and the length of the principal intestine would classify him as a carnivorous animal, but the bear is actually omnivorous.

Anyone who thinks that the bear is a slow and stupid animal has another guess coming. He is remarkably quick in his movements. He is also exceedingly cunning, a fact once dramatically illustrated to me. I had wounded a large cinnamon bear in the forest, and he ran from me up the side of the mountain. As the ground was slightly covered with snow, I could easily follow his trail. Presently among the trees ahead, I saw a large rock the size of a small house. The trail continued directly along the side of this rock. For some reason, unknown to me at the present time, I went below the trail looking about. Coming quietly to the other side of the rock I saw this big bear standing watching his back trail. If I had continued on that trail, I certainly would have been unexpectedly attacked. As it was, luck was on my side, and I shot and killed the bear.

One fall my friend, W. R. Coe, was visiting my ranch, and we decided on a camping and hunting trip in the mountains above my house. I had at that time a pack of dogs that I had expected to use in bear-hunting; so we took them along to try them out.

In a few days we came across a dead cow on which a bear had been feeding. I put the dogs on the trail of the bear, and with a tremendous enthusiasm they started off at full cry. In this mountainous region of high altitude, the air is very rarefied. Therefore, our horses were out of breath and exhausted before they had reached the top of the first divide. It is not practicable to hunt bears with dogs in a mountainous region, as there a horse cannot outrun a bear. On the plains or elsewhere, a horse can generally overtake both bear and dogs with a chance of the hunter's getting the bear.

Being mounted, we were forced to follow along the trail slowly and soon lost all sound of the dogs. We were eventually obliged to give up the pursuit. We hunted about the mountains during the day, crossed the divide, and early in the afternoon made camp in what is known as Boulder Basin.

While we prepared dinner one of my rangers rode into camp and gleefully announced, "Superintendent, I know where your bear is."

I said, "Well, then, you know more than I do. Where is he?"

"In a cave about ten miles over there," he replied, pointing to the other side of the canyon. "I was riding along and noticed that the dogs had caught the scent by the cave. I sent them in and pretty soon one of them came out, all cut up and bloody. Isn't that proof of your bear?"

I agreed that it was likely. But I knew that it would be impossible to get the bear out that day. It would surely be dark before we could get to the cave. I also knew that the bear would be sure to leave his retreat during the night. Whereupon I announced that I would give ten dollars to anyone who would go over to the cave and keep watch at its mouth to prevent the bear's escape.

"I'll go," yelled my cook, a young, enthusiastic fellow.

So he went off for his horse, came back to camp for the saddle, and with a bit of extra covering for the night started out with the ranger for the cave. There was snow on the ground and it promised to be a bitterly cold October night. My man Rush took the cook's place and was peeling potatoes. As he saw the cook riding into the cold night, he remarked, "About two o'clock in the morning he won't think it so damned romantic."

Camp was stirring early the next morning. We saddled our horses and started for the cave, having made sure of its location from the ranger the previous night. Good news for us—the bear had not come out!

The cave was up on the side of the canyon with a small, level platform about fifteen feet square in front of it. From this platform the rock rose almost perpendicularly. The mouth was about four feet wide and three feet high. We tried to send the dogs into the cave to rout out the bear, but after a few encounters they refused to return. The dogs having failed us, just what were we to do to get the bear out? I had brought an electric lantern along, so I said, "If anybody will go in with me and carry the light, I will accompany him and endeavor to get a shot at the bear."

There was some hesitation, but finally the ranger said he would go; so I gave him the light and, taking my rifle, we crawled into the cave on our hands and knees, side by side. The cave had evidently been an old watercourse. It went straight back for about fifteen feet and then turned abruptly to the right. We were near this turning and throwing the light on the rocks, when suddenly the bear's head appeared around the corner with a "woof!" The ranger was frightened and proceeded to withdraw as rapidly as possible, leaving me and the bear alone in the dark together. I concluded it was no place for Willie, so I also withdrew.

That startling glimpse of the bear in the cave reminds me of a German who was hunting near my ranch. Above him on the side of the mountain he saw a bear eating in the bushes. Only his hind quarters were visible. The hunter was greatly pleased at this opportunity of getting a bear and immediately started up the side of the hill through the sagebrush to get a shot. He crawled along very cheerfully and was intensely amused, saying to himself, "Vat a surprase I vill give dat bear!" Finally he was so near that the bear heard him and turned around suddenly with a "woof!" The German lost his nerve and started down the hill as fast as he could run, exclaiming, "Mein Gott, vot a difference it makes vich end he looks at you mit!"

Having failed to shoot the bear inside the cave, we went into a consultation as to the next proceeding and decided to try and smoke him out. We built a fire at the entrance to the cave with pine needles, which make a dense smoke, and as the wind was blowing towards the cave I thought the bear would be obliged to come out. I stood near the opening with my rifle ready to receive him.

The fire burnt down and no bear appeared. We renewed the fire with no better results. I then concluded that either there must be another exit to the cave through which the bear had escaped, or else he was suffocated by the smoke. The question was to find out whether the bear was there or not, so I called for volunteers. Our enthusiastic cook said at once he would go in. As he was a very poor cook, I gave my consent. So he took the electric light and entered the cave. In a short time he called out that the bear was dead.

We passed him in a rope, which he tied to the bear's foot and all getting hold of the end of the rope, we pulled him out of the cave. It turned out to be a large black bear. In following his track we had not known whether it was a black or a grizzly. Had it been a grizzly he certainly would have charged home and I might have been severely hurt. As it was we had smoked bear for dinner.

One day, when wandering amid the red stems of tall pine trees near the head of Piney, a small stream that flows into the Grey Bull close by my ranch house, I saw in the snow the tracks of three grizzly bears, which had lately passed that way. I started to follow their trail. Following fresh bear tracks is interesting. You surely know there are bears at the other end of the trail, but you do not know what they will do when you meet them, especially when there are three. So with a certain thrill I continued my quest for the known and the unknown. Their tracks wandered about among the trees and up the mountain. I followed carefully, keeping a sharp lookout on every side. The trail finally ended at the mouth of a cave. There were no tracks leaving, so I was sure of their whereabouts, but not at all sure how I was to get a shot.

I decided that I would try to smoke them out. I gathered some pine branches and, placing them in the entrance of the cave, applied a match. They cracked and burned, sending a dense smoke into the cave. I selected a spot just above the opening to await results.

The fire burned out. As the bears did not appear, I went down on a small, level space before the mouth of the cave with the intention of renewing the fire. Just then a bear came out, not six feet away.

I had my rifle ready and shot her in the center of the forehead. She dropped dead. This was fortunate, for in falling she so nearly filled the mouth of the cave that the other bears had difficulty in getting out. I was thus able to kill both of them as they crawled out.

Having been victorious in my engagement with the bears, I hit the trail down Piney leading to my ranch. A few miles above the ranch, alongside of Piney, there is an open meadow surrounded by groves of trees. The ground is slightly undulated. At one side, in the edge of a large grove, I saw a herd of some twenty elk, cows and calves. When I had ridden a little farther, so that I could barely see over the top of the ridge, I caught sight of a large mountain lion, crouching on the ground and crawling stealthily toward the elk, obviously in quest of his supper. As only my head had been exposed above the ridge, the mountain lion did not see me and I quickly withdrew. Dismounting, I took my rifle and walked to the top of the ridge. The lion was still stalking the elk. I took aim and fired. The creature was badly wounded, but jumped into a bunch of willows, which hid him from view. I approached this covert. It was not very large. I walked round it, attempting to get a view of the lion. I could hear him growling and groaning in the bushes but could not get a glimpse of him. Suddenly he charged out of his hiding place directly towards me. But a quick and lucky shot prostrated him. He was an unusually large mountain lion, measuring twelve feet from the nose to the tip of his tail; but a mountain lion is half tail.

I mounted my horse and continued on toward the ranch, intending to find someone to help me in skinning the lion. The trail took me through a grove of cottonwood trees and, looking up, I saw among the branches of a large tree above, two full-grown wildcats. I fired twice with my six-shooter and killed them both. The second cat was on a branch directly over the trail and came plumping down in front of my horse, which became so frightened that he turned and ran away with me. I had difficulty in keeping my seat but finally managed to arrest his flight and once more turned his head toward home. I stopped and picked up the two bobcats and tied them on the back of my saddle. I was soon at the ranch house, where the skins were dressed and prepared, and, later on, were sent to a taxidermist in New York to be made into rugs, along with the skins of the three bears and of the mountain lion, the trophies of one day's hunt. I might say in passing that although it closely resembles a lioness in form and color, the mountain lion does not really belong to the lion family but is a puma of the cat family.

I had always said and written that a bear will not attack a man unless molested, but it seems that there are exceptions to every rule. One day, while I was Forest Superintendent, I was making a tour of inspection. While riding along the bare ridge of a high mountain, I saw across the valley a large grizzly bear with her two cubs. I rode down the mountain and climbed up the other side until I reached a point near where I had seen the bear. I dismounted and tied my horse, and, taking my rifle, proceeded on foot up to the open plateau above me. Arriving there, I saw the bear on the opposite side of the plateau some hundred yards away.

She saw me at the same time, but instead of running away over the ridge as I expected, she charged directly at me, much to my surprise and contrary to all my former experience. I thought it was a bluff and waited to see what she would do. There was apparently no doubt in her mind, however, for she came rapidly toward me with her bristles raised, her mouth open, and with a cub boiling along on either side.

She was only fifteen steps distant when I shot and killed her. The cubs then ran away. I could easily have killed them, but as they were old enough to take care of themselves I let them go.

The bear is the most erratic of animals. No two of them act in the same way, and a man who has not killed more than half a dozen hasn't a very correct idea of their habits. I have known them, even when wounded, to run away as if the devil were after them, sometimes even leaving their cubs behind. At other times they exhibit perfect contempt for their enemy, man; and occasionally, as in this one instance, they charge without provocation.

The element of luck plays a large part in hunting, as in bridge. Unless you hold the cards you cannot win. Many years ago I was camped near the head of Piney with my friend, Mr. Claflin. Neither of us had killed a mountain sheep. My friend decided to take a small outfit and go up higher in the mountains in hope of securing a specimen of this rare animal. As there was a very picturesque view from our camp, I remained to paint a picture of it. My friend was absent about a week, and late one afternoon returned greatly pleased, bringing with him two heads of sheep as trophies. As we sat by the camp fire, he related his experience and I congratulated him on his success. The next morning I went down to the small stream that flowed through our camp and was brushing my teeth when I looked up and saw five mountain sheep on the side of the mountain not far from camp. I returned to my tent and exchanged my toothbrush for my rifle and went in pursuit of the sheep. I had gone only a short distance when I obtained an easy shot and brought down a fine ram, a larger and finer head than my friend had obtained during a week's hard work. Another time with the same friend I was hunting mountain goats north of what is known as Glacier Park. We had hunted for some time without success when one day going along a rocky trail we saw above and ahead of us a fine goat. We continued in this direction, when not far from the goat, the trail came to a point where a stream had worn the level rock to a perfectly smooth surface. Above the trail was a high cliff and a few feet below was a sheer drop of a hundred feet. When we arrived at that point I refused to go any farther, but my friend was more courageous and said he thought he could make it. The smooth surface was about fifty yards wide and I watched with apprehension my friend's careful progress, as a single misstep would have been death. He finally reached the other side safely and continued in the direction of the goat. In a short time I looked up and saw the goat coming in my direction, on a trail higher up on the west side. I waited until he was directly above me, when I shot and killed him, securing my first mountain goat.

For many years, I have hunted almost exclusively with a camera. It requires more skill to hunt successfully with a camera than a gun. One requires as much knowledge of woodcraft to track the animal to locate him, and then must approach to a near point to obtain a successful picture and also obtain a good light on the game. When one makes a successful shot with a rifle there is a bleeding, suffering animal dying on the ground. When one takes a shot with a camera he goes bounding off in abounding life. He goes home to Mrs. Elk and tells her how a cruel man tried to get him but he was too smart, and Mrs. Elk says, "Bless your heart, I always knew you were too smart for any animal with only two legs to get the best of you," and everybody is happy. I have succeeded in getting movies of every large animal in the Rocky Mountains as well as birds and small game.

At one time when hunting in Montana, I stopped overnight in a small town. The town consisted of a few straggling houses, a drinking and gambling saloon. That day a gambler had gotten into a dispute over a game of cards. The argument became hot, and the gambler drew his gun and killed his companion. They made a rude box of undressed boards and laid him in it. An immoral woman living in the town came and looked at him, and said "Poor Jim, he does not look comfortable." She then went and, taking from a bed her only pillow, came and placed it under his head and so, unmourned, they buried him.

CHAPTER XXII

CAMPING EXPERIENCES

On one of the hunting trips that I made with my friend, John Claflin, we left the train at Missoula, Montana, and there prepared for camp life. Our preparations consisted in buying four pack horses, two saddle horses, and a complete camping outfit, bedding, cooking utensils, and provisions, which were easily procured at this town. We then engaged a guide, cook, and horse-wrangler. After these preliminaries, we left Missoula and took the trail leading up the Missoula River, camping at night and marching during the day. We finally left the river, going up a narrow trail that led to an elevated plateau on which there was a prairie some miles in extent and surrounded by a dense growth of pine forest. We found a delightfully cool spring in the center of this plateau, and we made our permanent camp.

The plateau was known as Big Hole, and it was here that Major Gibbon had his fight with the Nez Percés Indians, led by Chief Joseph. In this battle the Major and nearly half of his command were killed. Then the soldiers withdrew to a slight rise in the pine forest and threw up breastworks. The Indians, secreted behind trees, got their range and were gradually picking them off and would probably have destroyed the entire outfit, but at that moment General Howard came up with two thousand soldiers. The Indians fled, going east through what is now Yellowstone Park, and were finally rounded up and captured by General Miles at a point near where my ranch now stands. The government has erected a monument here, and by this monument I saw a gruesome spectacle. Scattered over the ground, dug from their shallow graves by coyotes, were human bones, and white skulls grinning at their own ghastliness.

During the campaign of General Howard, the longest continuous march recorded in history was made, so he told me. He covered a distance of 2000 miles continuous march with his command of 2000 soldiers.

A few days after our encampment in this place, my friend, John, succeeded in killing a large bull moose. This was his first moose; so I decided to make a sketch of it for him. The next morning I packed up my paints, took a canvas with me, and, with my guide and John, set out on horseback to find the spot where he had killed the moose. We crossed the plateau, and after proceeding a distance among the pine trees, came to the moose lying in a small opening.

I at once put up my easel and started painting. John and the guide went to look for game. It was here that I lost my first opportunity of shooting a moose. While I was working on the picture, I noticed a moose coming toward me among the pine trees. I picked up my rifle, hoping to get a shot. But when I was about to shoot, I hesitated, as the head was behind a tree. The moose was so nearly the size and color of my horse, which was tied near the spot, that I feared to kill him instead. My opportunity was lost by this hesitation, as the moose rushed away and disappeared among the trees.

I worked on this picture the entire day, so absorbed that I scarcely noticed the flight of time, and did not see an approaching storm. But, towards dusk, the snow commenced falling. I gathered up my painting materials, saddled my horse, and started for camp.

When I reached the edge of the pine forest and regained the open plateau in the center of which our camp was located, I encountered a raging blizzard. Angry gusts of wind drove clouds of snow in my face that cut like sand. I could see but a few feet in any direction. It was then dark, and I did not have the slightest idea in which direction to look for camp. I was without extra clothing and with no food. To have passed the night on the open prairie would certainly have been attended with great risk. This unpleasant prospect was, however, avoided by the natural homing instinct of my horse. I gave him his head and hurried him along. Whenever his steps lagged, I would shake in the air the sketch I held in my hand. It may have been the canvas, or it may have been his idea of my sketch, but he would immediately start off on a run. Thus we proceeded over this wilderness of trackless white. The dense snow restricted any possible view, but finally, through the driving storm, I saw a glimmer of red. In a short time the horse had brought me to camp and I was seated by the camp fire, surrounded by anxious companions. It was certainly a great relief to find shelter, warmth, and the smell of frying bacon.

At another time, Claflin and I were hunting near the top of the Rockies along the Canadian border in the Blackfoot reservation, now known as Glacier Park. We had gone to that locality to hunt mountain goat, a rare animal that I had never had the opportunity of shooting. One morning, just after finishing breakfast, I was surveying the surrounding mountains through my field glasses. Far in the distance, near the top of an adjacent mountain, I saw a small white speck. It was so white that it undoubtedly was either an animal or a patch of snow. I watched for a long time and finally saw it move. It was obviously not snow. So, mounting my horse and taking my guide with me, I started for that distant spot. The trail was exceedingly difficult, as the mountainside was very steep and rugged.

I climbed a long time before I reached the place where I had seen the goat, but finally, near the top of the mountains, I saw him standing on the peak of some rocks. It was a peculiar formation, for situated in the middle of a high plateau was a ridge of rocks rising over a hundred feet from the surrounding level. At either end of this "hogback" was a peak of rocks, and the goat, when I saw him, was standing on one of these. I climbed up the ridge to get a better shot, but when I arrived at that point the goat had descended. Along the top of the ridge was a well-worn trail that he had evidently used for a long time as he marched back and forth from one point to another to watch for danger. I went to the other end of the ridge, and there, directly below me, was one of the largest mountain goats I have ever seen. He looked up at me, his face framed by a long, white beard, somewhat comical and reminding me of a well-known face. I shot and killed him, and then proceeded to remove his hide. That completed, we started on our return to camp.

Since then I have killed a number of goats but never one that could compare with this in size. When my guide, who was not a very tall man, folded the skin by the middle over his shoulders, the head and tail touched the ground behind him.

We climbed down the mountainside till we came to the trees where we had tied our horses. It was then dark, and we were a long way from camp; ahead of us a most difficult trail, not only to find, but dangerous to follow. At one point where it was impossible to ride, I dismounted and was leading my horse when I made a misstep and fell over the precipice beside the trail. Fortunately, I fell in a river just below, which broke my fall. Had I fallen on the rocks, the result might have been different! My guide, who was ahead, stopped my horse and helped me to mount again. It was quite black and I was wet, hungry, and tired, but we still struggled forward looking for camp. I was very doubtful as to its locality until I heard a rifle shot. My friend, John Claflin, being anxious about our late return, had been occasionally firing a shot. This sound brought us safely back to camp, after a strenuous climb of fourteen hours up and down the mountainside.

Once, when camping at a very pretty spot near the Anderson Fork, I decided a short time before sunset to get a mess of trout for dinner. I put together my light trout rod, a very fine one that had been given me, and fished along the edge of the stream, getting but few rises. Presently I saw a pool on the other side of the stream that looked more propitious. The river was too deep for me to cross on foot. My horse, saddled, was standing near; I mounted, carrying my fishpole in my hand, and started to cross the stream. It was a windy, blustery day, and by some unfortunate accident the hook at the end of the line caught on the horse's haunch. He started to run and buck. At a furious rate he bucked me all over the camp ground, much to the amusement of the cook and horse-wrangler, who stood there laughing as if they would split their sides. I did not see anything amusing about it; in fact, I thought they had a very queer sense of humor! I had difficulty in remaining in the saddle and was obliged to drop the fishing rod, which then dragged behind the horse, increasing his fright. I finally did get him quieted down so that the cook could come up and take him by the bridle. I descended to terra firma, but my beautiful trout rod was completely destroyed.

I made up my mind then and there never again to try to land a horse on a six-ounce trout rod!

Rattlesnakes are very numerous in Wyoming. Sometimes, when driving in tent pegs and arranging camp in the tall grass, one may come on one of these intruders. One day I was seated on a rock having my lunch when I heard the vibration of a rattlesnake's tail. Somewhat startled, as I knew from the sound it was near by, I jumped to my feet and looked around. I saw a large rattlesnake coiled up under the overhanging rock upon which I had been sitting. I immediately killed him with my six-shooter.

While I was in camp at the place near Anderson Fork of which I have just spoken, a partner of one of my guides told me of an adventure that he had just had with a rattlesnake. He said that he was riding over a plain and saw a rattlesnake. He dismounted. As he approached, the snake started to crawl into a hole in the ground. He caught it by the tail to pull it out. At that moment his horse, which he had been holding by the bridle, gave a jump. He turned his head to speak to the horse and just then the snake doubled back, striking his fangs into the back of his hand. He did not die from the poison, but his hand withered up and became crippled and useless.

One day I was riding in the Forest Reserve with a ranger following me. He suddenly called. I looked around and saw him with his feet drawn up to the saddle. His horse was standing rigid with his feet far apart.

"What is the matter?" I asked.

"Come back and see!"

I turned my horse and rode back. There directly under his horse, I saw a large timber rattler coiled and ready to strike. Pulling out my six-shooter and taking careful aim, I put a bullet through him. He was decapitated as cleanly as though it had been done with a knife.

As the snake remained coiled, the ranger said, "But you did not hit him!"

I told him to get off and see for himself. He did so, looked at the snake, and said, "Gosh!"

There are many false beliefs about snakes. One is that snakes have power to charm birds. Another false belief is that the milk snake draws milk from the cow. The snake has not sufficient suction power to draw milk, and then, too, his sharp curved teeth would inflict such pain that the cow would soon get rid of him. From childhood I have heard of the hoop snake, which takes his tail in his mouth and rolls over the ground like a hoop. I once saw a composition written by a small boy. It said: "A little boy saw a snake that had his tail in his mouth and was rolling over the ground like a hoop. He thought it was a hoop that had gotten away from another little boy and picked up a stick to drive it home. You may think this is not true, but it is. I saw it myself and the little boy was my father."

Most of the poisonous snakes in this country are found in the Crotalidae family. They are divided into three species: the rattlesnake *(Crotalus horridus)*, the moccasin *(Agkistrodon piscivorus)*, and the copperhead *(Agkistrodon mokasen)*. There is only one other poisonous snake, the coral snake *(Micrurus fulvius)*, found only on the Mexican boundary (this is wrongly called the blood snake); the poison of the coral snake is different from that of the viper family; it acts directly on the nerve centers, while the poison of the rattler is carried by the circulatory system, destroying the red corpuscles and paralyzing the heart.

There are fifteen varieties of rattler, the largest being the diamond-black timber rattler, some eight feet in length, while the smallest is the Wilton rattler, only fifteen inches long. Although we have a dense population and poisonous snakes are numerous in all our states, except Maine, New Hampshire, and Vermont, but few accidents occur, careful investigation proving that less than one hundred accidents happen in a year.

A poisonous snake has two distinctive features: its head is larger than its neck (the only exception is the coral snake, whose head and neck are the same size), and it has what is known as the adder pit, a small hollow between the nose and the eye, an indentation just over the poisonous fangs. This is true of snakes found in America and does not apply to the snakes of other continents.

Some very peculiar incidents have occurred while hunting. From the camp at Anderson Fork I one day rode up in the mountain in quest of game. I had followed along a ridge for several miles when I saw a large buck deer. I shot at him, but, as he was running, the bullet struck a spot too far back of his heart to stop him at once. He continued his flight and I took up his trail, marked for some distance by drops of blood. These finally disappeared, making it impossible to follow his trail any farther; so I never expected to see my deer again. Late in the day I returned, and, to my surprise, found a deer hanging in the camp. This proved to be the very deer I had shot at. It had continued its course down the mountain and had run between the cook and the camp fire, dropping dead a few feet beyond.

When returning to the ranch I crossed over the high divide between the Wind River and Grey Bull, on the top of which there were several feet of snow. Snow was still falling. As it had come suddenly, the ground underneath was not frozen. Just as we crossed the divide, one of our pack horses mired down in a mudhole hidden by the snow. We removed his pack, attached several ropes to him, and, with the other ends around the horns of our saddles, we succeeded in pulling him out. Doing all this in a snow-storm at low temperature was difficult and disagreeable. When we had extricated him and replaced his pack, Westly, one of the cowboys, brushed the snow from the top of a rock, sat down, and said, "I wish mother had all her little boys at home tonight and I was sitting on her knee."

We soon mounted our horses and were strung along the narrow trail, wending our way in Indian file down the mountainside. Westly, bringing up the rear, began lustily to sing the cowboy song:

> Perhaps you have a mother,
> Likewise a sister, too,
> An' maybe you've a sweetheart
> To weep and mourn for you;
>
> If that be your situation,
> Although you'd like to roam,
> I'd advise you by experience
> You had better stay at home.

One day I was riding the range with some of my cow-boys when I came upon a calf that had been killed the night before. The boys said it was the work of a bear. I doubted that, as it did not appear to me like bear's work. However, I sent down to the ranch and got a bear trap. Building a V-shaped pen of logs around the dead calf, I placed the trap at the mouth of the pen. I also put at the same spot a camera arranged to take a picture by flashlight. There was a copper wire from the camera across the opening of the pen. Any animal entering the pen would strike this wire, set off the flashlight, and operate the camera. Having completed these arrangements, I returned to the ranch to await develop-ments. The next morning I found that the trap was not sprung, but the camera was. When I developed the plate, to my surprise I found that a large wolf had taken his own photograph, as shown in the illustration.

One November day I was hunting for deer, and came upon a male deer standing alone in the snow. Three times I shot. He did not fall! I approached to find him dead. He was standing in two feet of snow and the hard crust held him upright.

I was riding on through a terrific snowstorm. I had descended a hill along an edge of trees to the leeward of the wind, coming soon to an open glade below. Above the roar of the wind I heard a curiously familiar sound, and turned my unwilling horse in that direction. Through the sheets of drifting snow I saw two bull elk in a desperate fight. They had evidently been fighting for a considerable time, as the snow had been packed under their feet to form a natural arena.

No human prize-fight could be more thrilling. Here no money stakes, no gambler's odds. Theirs the only prize coveted in the animal world—the domination of a herd of cows after the killing of a rival male. Here no blazing lights to disclose the fighter's finesse. Driving snow was now a silver screen and antlered bodies a silhouette; again it swirled them into a gray confusion of lines and mass. No hoarse thousands here to cheer, to curse, to go mad with bloodlust. No frenzied McNamee at the microphone. I alone watched the fight. Two bulls in nature's wild, primitive ring; now a feint, a blow parried; again an attack, a clinch. Man knows little more about the technique of battle than these strong-limbed, bloody-eyed fighters.

For a half-hour round they fought, brute strength their only referee. At last one terrific crash of antlers, and one

TIMBER WOLF, TAKEN BY FLASHLIGHT

bull emerged the victor. Then the proud victor raised his head and trumpeted forth the clear challenge of the bull elk, that like a bugle note vibrated and echoed amid the mountain peaks.

At another time I happened to be riding in the mountains above my ranch when, alongside a small lake, I saw the record of a fight between two elk as clearly as if it had been written by hand. Beside the lake was a grassy glade, and beyond that a pine forest. The conflict had taken place in the open, and judging from the way the grass was trampled, it had been witnessed by a large group of cow elks.

Apparently the struggle had continued for a long time, until their horns became so interlocked that they could not separate them. The larger bull had broken the neck of the smaller bull. Then, with horns still interlocked, he had dragged the dead body about while seeking for grass, but finally dropped from exhaustion. There he lay until he died of starvation.

I came upon their bodies shortly after this tragedy had occurred. I removed their heads and had them mounted. They now adorn my studio and can be seen in the upper right-hand corner above the sixteenth-century doorway, as shown in the illustration. Directly beneath them and over the old Dutch clock is the head of a chamois killed and presented to me by the Prince of Monaco.

While I have done considerable hunting, and, I believe, killed every kind of game on this continent except musk ox, I have never wantonly taken life. I have never killed an elk, deer, mountain sheep, or antelope unless it was to secure an unusually fine pair of horns for my collection, or unless I was in need of meat. In recent years I have hunted only predatory animals, such as bears, wolves, mountain lions, and coyotes, that are destructive of other kinds of game.

One summer I went into a remote part of the Rockies on a hunting trip. The season for big game opened on September 1st. The previous day Rush and I made camp at a propitious spot and started out on horses to look over the surroundings. We had gone only a short distance when we saw a herd of eighteen elk directly before us. Rush urged me to shoot one. I refused; since, as assistant state game warden, I was enforcing the laws on others, I did not want to break them myself. Rush was greatly disgruntled. And, strange to say, we hunted a long time before we had another opportunity to shoot elk.

We were returning to camp one evening and had reached an elevation where we stopped for a while to rest our horses. Before us, far to the westward, dramatized by a colorful sunset, was one of the most extensive and glorious views I have ever seen. I sat on my horse spellbound and, turning to Rush, I said, "Have you ever seen anything so beautiful?"

"No, I have not," he crisply replied, "but you can't live on beautiful scenery."

Our provisions were indeed getting low. We had no fresh meat in camp and my guide thought a meal without meat was no meal at all. I resolved to take a hunt by myself early the next day in the hope of replenishing our larder.

I was up before daylight and started out on foot for my hunt. It had rained during the night, but the sun came up clear and bright.

The morning had finished its toilet and the raindrops glistened like diamonds on the tips of the leaves.

The arms of the sky were full of white clouds and like ladies' lingerie were hung out to dry.

However, I had not come out to admire the beauties of nature but in quest of food.

I proceeded cautiously over the wet herbs and through the sweet, hushed forests, looking in every direction in quest of game. I came to a slight rise which led to an opening among the trees. Before me lay a small grassy meadow sprinkled with wild flowers, framed with a border of stately trees, and flooded with the light of the rising sun. My heart leaped as I saw in the center of the opening a graceful black-tail deer feeding. Truly it was a scene to thrill the soul of an artist. But I was a hunter in search of food. I raised my gun, took careful aim, and was crooking my finger on the trigger when a pretty little spotted fawn, that I had not seen, got up from the tall grass and commenced to draw nourishment from its mother. The doe turned her head and lavished upon her offspring the tenderness of a mother. I did not press the trigger but lowered my gun and quietly withdrew without disturbing them. After a long walk through the forest of primeval trees I reached camp and ate bacon for breakfast. There is something in maternity that appeals to the heart of every man.

CHAPTER XXIII

THE STORY OF WAB

ONE year when Mr. W. R. Coe of New York visited my ranch we amused ourselves with horseback riding and fishing about the ranch for a time; then we decided to go up in the mountains to hunt big game. We brought in the saddle and pack horses, selected our camp outfit, and left the ranch. Our party consisted of my friend Coe, Lieutenant Boyd, a forest ranger, my ranch foreman, Rush, a horse-wrangler, cook, Johnny Goff, as guide, and myself.

Johnny Goff was a guide of unusual character, a most reliable person, a remarkable hunter of great experience, an interesting companion, and had been a guide of President Roosevelt on numerous occasions. I had a number of delightful hunting trips with him; finally I appointed him forest ranger, and detailed him especially to hunt mountain lions on the Yellowstone Reserve. At that time, mountain lions were quite numerous on the range. They are the most destructive of predatory animals, not only of stock, but of wild game. One season, in the Jackson Hole country, they killed every colt in that section, and also killed a number on my ranch.

After I had appointed Goff, I received the following letter from Colonel Roosevelt, which shows what an interest he took in all American citizens from the highest to the lowest:

THE WHITE HOUSE
WASHINGTON

My dear Mr. Anderson:

I have been much pleased to learn of what you are going to do with Johnny Goff. He is a personal friend of mine, and I have entire confidence in him. I should like to have him given the privilege of taking hunting parties into the forest reserve for bear and mountain lion, as well as any other game that can properly be killed. If he can be allowed to take parties to hunt lion in the park, I shall be glad, as it is perfectly safe to have him do so. He would only take into the park people whom he could absolutely trust, and the only gun that would be taken would be his own, which he would pack. I shall esteem it a personal favor if all that can properly be done for Goff you will see is done.

When are you coming to Washington? I should like to have you take lunch or dinner with me when you do.

Sincerely yours,

THEODORE ROOSEVELT

We had been camping and hunting for a short time up in the mountain and had made a pleasant camp on Anderson Fork, a branch of the Grey Bull River. Here we had plenty of wood, grass for the horses, and water; in fact, all the necessities of an ideal camp. The next morning Mr. Coe and Johnny Goff started off to hunt for mountain sheep in an easterly direction to what is known as Venus Basin. Lieutenant Boyd and I rode up Anderson Fork in the bright sunlight, but we hunted without success. After lunch, however, as we rode our horses farther up the creek, we came across the track of a deer and started to follow it. During this quest Boyd and I became separated. I hunted for him for a time, firing off my gun to attract his attention, but he did not appear. In the meantime the sky had become overcast, and presently it began to snow. It was getting late, and as I was a long distance from camp, I decided to return. Boyd was on horseback and perfectly acquainted with that part of the mountains. He had his saddle blanket, which would keep him from being too uncomfortable in case he had to remain out all night.

I arrived at camp just before dark, and found that neither Coe nor Boyd had returned. I waited for some time and then had my dinner alone. When ten o'clock came, with still no word of my companions, I sought the shelter of my tent and the warmth of my blankets. The snow had been falling steadily and had soon accumulated on the top of my tent to such depth that its weight, abetted by the force of the wind, broke one of the tent poles, and the tent with its mass of snow fell upon me. I barely managed to wriggle my way to the lower part of the tent, where the other pole was still standing. Under this slight shelter I passed the remainder of the night. Later I wrote some lines about my experience, the last verse of which reads:

> Crash, snap, bang! I hear the pole give way.
> Flip, flap, flop! The tent begins to sway.
> What is this dreadful weight I feel upon my heart?
> A ton of cold, cold snow had tumbled in the dark.
> I crawl, I wriggle, and in my dreadful plight,
> I whisper to my dog, "What a hell of a night!"

When I crawled out of my tent the next morning, neither Boyd nor Coe had yet appeared, and it was not until nine o'clock that Boyd rode into camp. I remarked that in spite of his night's experience he was looking very spruce. "Perhaps that's because I slept under a spruce tree," he replied.

Mr. Coe did not get back until nearly noon and had passed a most uncomfortable night, as he and Johnny Goff were without food or covering. . . . They could not go to sleep, or they would have been in danger of freezing. They kept a small fire burning under a pine tree, and stood before it all night. They were afoot and had a long tramp back to camp through the snow.

As the snow was then too deep for us to continue hunting and was still falling, I decided to break camp and strike the trail for the ranch. I left my men to pack up the outfit, and with Coe and Boyd mounted our saddle horses and started back for the Palette Ranch. It was a long, hard ride through the deep snow, and we did not reach home until dark.

After dinner we sat down before my large fireplace with its blazing fire of logs. The cheer and warmth within were a great relief after our experiences and a decided contrast to the storm raging outside. Coe lighted a cigar, but had taken only a few puffs when the cigar fell to the floor from his hand. He was asleep. I concluded that bed would be the proper place for all of us. We slept late into the next day, and when we arose were all in the best of health, not having suffered in the least from exposure.

Mr. Coe was so delighted with the ranch and its surroundings that he told me he, too, would like to have a ranch in the locality. I had loaned Buffalo Bill some money, and had taken an option on one of his ranches called the Carter Ranch. I showed the ranch to Mr. Coe, and as he seemed pleased with it, I turned the option over to him. I was delighted to have as a neighbor not only one of my particular friends, but a man as well possessed with the soul of honor, and of many other estimable qualities. He exercised the option and with considerable expense and taste has made his property one of the most interesting ranches in Wyoming.

One summer Ernest Thompson Seton, whose animal stories are known throughout the world, visited the ranch, accompanied by his charming wife, Grace Thompson Seton, who is also a brilliant writer. During their stay, I told Mr. Seton about an unusually large grizzly bear that had been frequenting the country about my ranch for many years and had been most destructive to my cattle. There was but one marauder; I knew this by the track, which measured thirteen inches in width. Bears' feet often vary in size, like women's; I have killed large bears with small feet, and small bears with large feet. I knew that this was an unusually large bear not only by the size of his track but by the depth it would sink down into the soft earth.

I told Seton about this bear, and some of my other experiences bear-hunting, and, with his literary ability, he wove them into an entertaining story called "Wab, or the Biography of a Grizzly," and dedicated it to the Palette Ranch. In this account he had Wab deliberately commit suicide in Death Valley. This is poetic license, as Wab met a different end.

As Wab had killed a number of my cattle (one day his trail led me by the carcasses of five cows he had killed) and was rather an expensive boarder, I decided to get rid of him. Wab only came down to the ranch in the early spring and pulled out usually in the month of April. He probably went over to Yellowstone Park, only twenty-five miles distant, to live on the refuse of hotels. Although I did not usually go to my ranch until midsummer or fall, I decided to make an exception and go in the month of May in the hopes of having an interview with Wab.

That year, as I have earlier related, Mayor John Purroy Mitchell was asked to open the Universal Exhibition in San Francisco and on his way out I invited him to visit my ranch. The Mayor was a good sport, and was delighted at the prospect of getting a shot at a bear. We arrived at my ranch one afternoon about four o'clock. My foreman told me that a bear had killed a cow the night before, two miles above the ranch house. Knowing that a bear will often return a second time to the place of his prey, I thought I was going to be fortunate in giving the Mayor a shot at the bear immediately.

A bear is a nocturnal animal, spending his day hiding in some deep shade of the forest and coming out only at dusk in search of food. Just before sunset, therefore, we mounted our horses and rode up the valley to the spot where the bear had killed the cow.

We found the carcass partly eaten; so the Mayor and I concealed ourselves behind a near-by rock to await his coming. But our waiting was in vain. The veil of night came down, and no bear appeared. After a bear has gorged himself the night of his kill, he seldom shows up the following night, but almost invariably returns the second evening. So I was not discouraged at his non-appearance, feeling sure that we would be successful the next evening. On that day, unfortunately, Mayor Mitchell was taken with one of the dreadful headaches to which he was subject, and for two days was not able to leave the house. As I was anxious that the Mayor should kill the bear I did not go to the bait. When Mr. Mitchell was able to ride out with me, we discovered that the cow had been completely devoured. And not by one, but by three bears. I then decided to put out another bait.

My house is situated on a small stream called the Piney, the dearest little stream that ever tumbled down a mountain-side. It rises in a large spring some six miles above my ranch and, tumbling down over the clean boulders, is aërated, and makes the most delightful drinking water I have ever discovered, as cold as ice-water all summer long. About five miles above my ranch a game trail comes down the side of the mountain and crosses Piney. It is frequently used by bears. On the north side of Piney at that point is a small, open meadow. There I decided to place my bait. I had an old horse, no longer of any use, and as bears are more fond of horse meat than any other kind, I decided to use the horse for that purpose. I directed one of the cowboys to take the horse to that spot, shoot him, and let me know if the carcass was found by bears. On the second day he told me that a bear was using the bait. We had an early dinner that day, and the Mayor and I rode up Piney, secreting ourselves behind some sagebrush a short distance from the bait.

Snow covered the ground. The air was cold. But we patiently waited in hopes of a visit from the bear. Finally just before dark I saw an immense bear which I recognized as Wab coming directly down the creek towards us. I waited until he was not more than fifty yards away, and, turning to the Mayor, who was behind me, whispered, "Jack, he's coming."

The Mayor rose to his feet as if he were going to make an address, and said, "Where?"

The bear saw him, jumped behind some willow brush and disappeared. He never saw him again.

We returned the following evening, but the bear, having been frightened, did not return again to the bait until after dark. A few days after, the Mayor was obliged to go to San Francisco, where he was to open the World's Fair, and, I am sorry to say, never got his bear.

I was very anxious to get rid of Wab, and, as I did not see him come out before dark, I decided to trap him. I do not consider trapping a very manly sport, and would not have resorted to it in this instance had not the bear been so destructive of my cattle. I set the bear trap beside the carcass. A bear trap is a large steel trap weighing some forty pounds, with a chain and a ring, by which it is attached to a movable log. If it were not attached to a movable object, when the bear first placed his foot in it, he would certainly tear loose; but as the log is movable, this does not happen. I carefully placed the trap beside the bait, covered it with leaves and grass so that it was invisible to the eye, and returned to the ranch.

The following morning with great curiosity and anticipation, I returned to see if the bear had been at the bait. I found that he had been there. And now I am going to tell you something that I would not have believed, had I not seen it myself. The trap had been sprung! It was in the same spot, and the jaws merely closed. There was no hair in it, and not the slightest evidence as to how the trap had been sprung.

That day I placed a second trap on the other side of the bait, carefully concealed. On returning the following morning, I found that both traps were closed. I was somewhat discouraged but again set both traps. When I returned the next day, one trap was sprung. The other, having been exposed to the rain and the damp air, had become rusted so that, although the pedal had been pushed down, the jaws had failed to close. But, strange to relate, the bear had turned the trap over so that the teeth were on the ground. Thus, if the trap did close, it would do no harm. This sounds incredible but it is absolutely true.

As I found that the bear was too cunning to be trapped, and the carcass was nearly consumed, I decided to watch for him again at dusk. The following evening I went to the bait, and hiding behind some sagebrush twenty-five yards from the carcass, I waited. As I have said, there was a small meadow between me and the stream, and directly opposite, on the other side of the stream, the game trail went up the mountainside among the pine trees.

I waited and waited, and had almost given up hope of seeing the bear, when I looked up on the mountainside, and there between the openings in the trees I saw two bears wandering about, gradually making their way down the mountain. As it turned out, one of them was a female bear;

the other, who was following her, was Wab. This love affair was the cause of his destruction.

Presently the female bear came down the trail, rushed up to the bait, and commenced to eat. She was only twenty-five yards away and I could easily have killed her then and there, but I waited in hopes of the larger bear joining her. The female bear at that particular point evidently got a whiff of air and scented my presence, as she threw up her head and started on a run across the meadow, splashed across the stream and headed up the trail. I then saw it was my last chance, and, taking careful aim, cut loose. The bullet went true, and she rolled down dead at the bottom of the trail.

I then saw Wab crossing a small opening among the trees at a fast walk. I took aim and fired, and going up there I found the bear dead only a few yards from the spot I had shot at him. I rather congratulated myself that I had killed two grizzlies moving, one 100 yards and the other 150 yards distant, in two shots. This was the last chapter in Wab's history of destruction. His skin now decorates my studio. During the morning of the same day I had been successful in killing two other grizzlies; a total of four grizzlies in one day.

CHAPTER XXIV

A VISIT TO ALASKA

I COULD fill a book with my bear experiences. I have killed thirty-nine grizzlies, besides numerous black, brown, and Alaskan bears. But I shall relate only one more bear story. I had occasion to visit Alaska several times because of my responsibilities as president of a gold mine on the Nome peninsula. But one of my most interesting trips was a hunting expedition to this sportsman's paradise, where game of all kinds is everywhere in abundance.

In Seattle I engaged a guide by the name of L. L. Bales, a well-known hunter who, by the way, had written some articles on bear-hunting. With our camping outfit, we boarded the steamer. The officers of the Alaska Steamship Company extended the courtesy of transportation to me, and agreed to land me at any point desired on the coast of Alaska. As my destination, I decided on Stephenov Bay near the end of the Aleutian peninsula.

Arriving near Alaska, we sailed for several days along the coast, and a more inhospitable coast I have never seen, —no trees in sight, only high, rugged, snow-covered mountains. Finally we arrived in Stephenov Bay, and my outfit was sent ashore in a small boat. We made camp at the mouth of a small valley, which in Alaska is called a tundra. A small stream came down the valley at this point, bringing us fresh water.

I hunted in that locality for several days, but did not see

any bears, although I did find numerous tracks and many bones of salmon off which the bears had been feeding. One day, however, I killed a caribou that furnished fresh meat for the camp. It was a fat young cow and made excellent food. Finding no bears there, Bales and I moved camp up ten miles to the head of the tundra.

There were trails leading across the tundra two feet deep and two feet wide made by bears going to and from their fishing ground, where probably they have been wandering back and forth for hundreds of years. Bears are exceedingly fond of fish, and during the season when the salmon are going up the river to spawn, they catch many of them. It is no easy matter for a large animal like the bear to catch fish in the stream. They are, however, very clever and successful fishers. A bear will go into a stream, and, to steady himself, put his paw around a large rock that protrudes above the water. His other paw is placed below the surface. In this position he remains quietly until he sees a salmon approaching in the clear water. He then slips his paw beneath the salmon and, with a quick flip, tosses it onto the shore. Rushing after it, he grabs it in his mouth and kills it.

The stream on which our camp lay was about twenty feet wide. At places there were ripples where the water was only a few inches deep, running swiftly over pebbles and stones, to gather in deep pools. A bear would place her cubs in the ripples above a pool, and then jump in the deep pool with such great splashing and turmoil as to frighten the salmon. To escape, the salmon would swim up the ripples. There in the shallow water the cubs could easily catch them in their mouths and carry them to the shore, where the old bear would join them and with her paws strip the flesh from the bones, giving delicate morsels to the cubs. While this may sound like a "fish story," it is a bear fact!

Bear-hunting in Alaska differs from the same sport in any other part of the world. The bear passes the day buried in the snow, far up on the mountainside, but early in the morning comes down the mountain in search of food. Arriving at the base of the mountain on the tundra, he eats the grass and young sprouts, and salmon. He then returns up the mountainside and finds a spot on the snow where he passes the day. You watch him through your glasses, and marking down the spot where he stops, you proceed to climb up the mountain, and if not killed by a fall or an avalanche of snow, you can easily obtain a shot at the bear.

We prepared our dinner, and entering our tent, crawled into our fur sleeping bags, where we were soon fast asleep. The next morning at an early hour I awakened Bales. (Daylight in that part of Alaska and at that season comes about two o'clock in the morning.) Bales proceeded to dress and then climbed up a bank to a high ridge that gave him a commanding view of the surrounding country.

I returned to my warm sleeping bag and slept on until aroused by a call from Bales. From a high point above, Bales was yelling and waving his arms around through the perfectly good air. Surmising that he had spotted game, I secured my rifle and soon joined him. He pointed out a small black speck on the other side of the valley coming down over the snow. From where we were it looked like a black flea, but on examining it with my field glasses I saw that it was indeed a large bear. He continued down the side of the mountain, zigzagging along, at times sitting down on his haunches and sliding, until finally he reached level ground. The tundra at that point was about a mile wide, largely covered with black alder brush. The bear entered the brush and could be distinctly seen, as, at that early period in May, there were but few leaves on the bushes, and the ground was covered with snow.

He wandered about for some time eating the sprouts, but was not true to schedule, for instead of returning up the mountainside, he lay down on the snow among the bushes. I zigzagged down over the snow from my high position and, reaching the tundra, continued to the edge of the jungle in which he was hidden.

"What are you going to do?" Bales asked when we reached the edge.

"I am going into the brush in the hopes of getting a shot at the bear."

"That is not courageous but foolhardy!" he said.

"Well, I am hunting bear," I said, "and I see no other way of getting this one."

He positively refused to go with me, much to my annoyance, as never before had a guide refused to follow me. Whereupon, I entered the jungle alone. It was a most difficult stalk, as the snow, two feet deep, was covered by a hard crust. This would occasionally break through, and I would go down as though I had broken a leg. Sometimes I would accidentally break off a dead branch of the alders, or startle a flock of ptarmigans, which would give forth a loud cry that sounded like somebody saying, "Come here! Come here!" making so much noise that I was afraid they would drive the bear out of the jungle. But perhaps their wild notes were not a new sound to him; at all events, I continued my quest.

Finally I reached the locality that seemed to be near the spot where I had seen the bear. I had marked his position by two high rocks on either side of the valley. The alder brushes were about fourteen to fifteen feet high, with trunks six inches in diameter. These grew zigzagging in every direction, making a network so dense that it was difficult to see more than a short distance. I stood looking about the bushes for the bear when he suddenly got up not more than

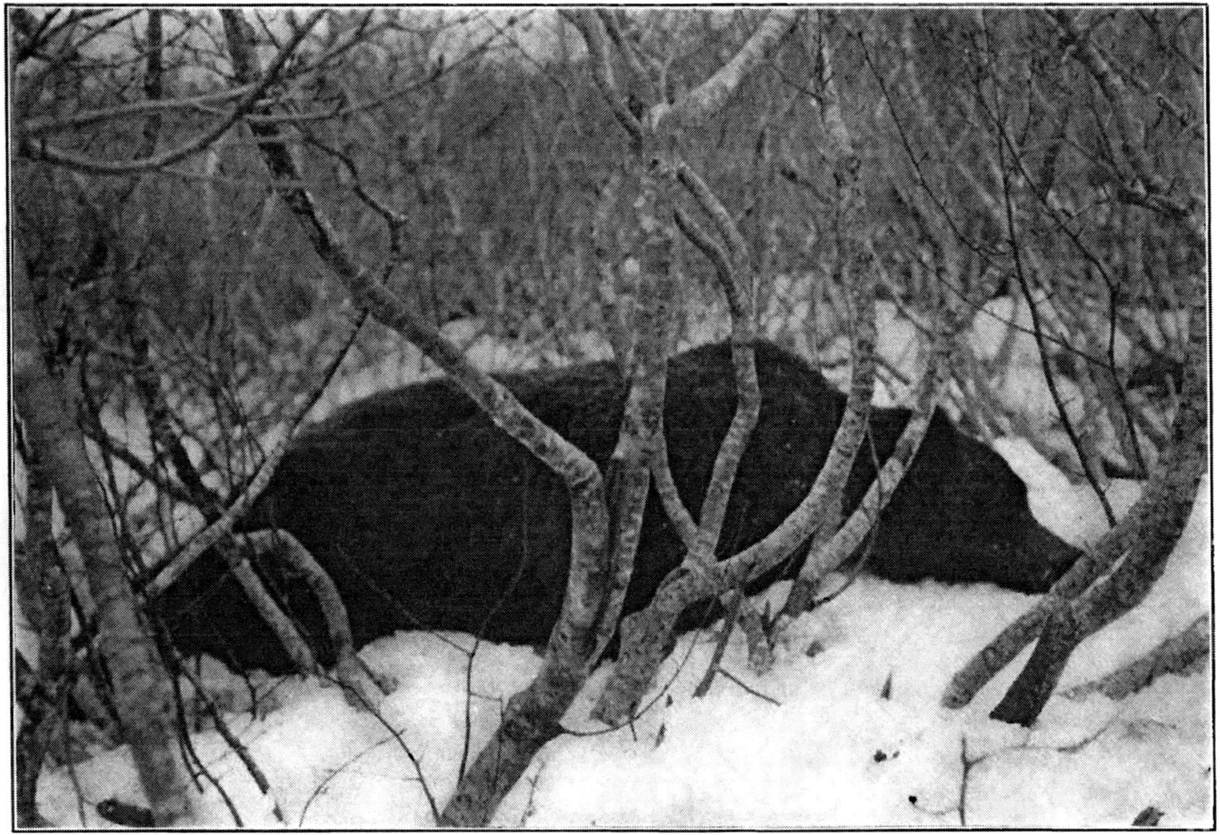

BEAR KILLED IN ALASKA

twenty-five yards from where I was standing. I could distinctly catch his outline, one side of his head, and one eye, which was watching me, but I could not make out any vital spot to shoot at. There was an opening about a foot in diameter through which I distinctly saw his hip. I knew I was taking some risk of merely wounding him at that short distance, but I also knew that if I did not shoot then, I would never get a shot at all. I took careful aim at the hip bone, and cut loose. One would have thought a cyclone had struck the bushes. Giving out a roar, the bear came directly towards me. I had broken his hip, but he could come all right on three legs. I had time to get in just two shots before he was directly upon me. But my last shot to his head was fatal, and he dropped dead at my feet.

I waited to hear from Bales, and after some time I heard him call. I yelled, and presently Bales made his appearance, saying, "Anderson, why didn't you holler?"

"I thought you heard the noise," I replied.

"I did," he said, "but I did not know what had happened."

He evidently was not going to take any chance of meeting a wounded bear. When he looked down on the immense brute lying upon my empty shells, he slapped me on the back and said, "By God, Anderson, you shook hands with Hell that time, all right."

The bear was so large we could not turn him over to skin him, so I sent Bales to our lower camp for the cook. When he arrived we proceeded to skin the bear. Skinning a bear is no easy job. The skin is not loose and easy to pull off, like that of an elk or a deer, but, like a hog's hide, grows fast to the body. All of it has to be cut away with a knife, and care must be taken not to cut the skin. Finally we succeeded in skinning (or more accurately, "unskinning") the bear, and the three of us then packed the hide to the boat, and, putting our camp outfit with it, paddled down the stream to our main camp. This skin now hangs in my studio.

The captain of the steamship had promised to stop for me in three weeks on his return trip. I was anxious that he should not forget to do so, as otherwise it would have been impossible for me to get away from that remote spot. I had only a small boat, making it impossible to leave by water, and back of me and around in every direction were hundreds of miles of snow-capped mountains without an inhabitant. Welcome indeed, then, was the sound of the familiar whistle and the sight of the steamer coming up the bay. They sent in a small boat, and we were soon safely aboard and on our way to New York.

Shortly after my arrival, I went to Washington, and while there, with the Assistant Secretary of State, Robert Bacon, called upon President Roosevelt. He was in his office surrounded by many visitors. He was talking to an ambassador, and with a few appropriate words then discussed some important political point with a senator or representative, turning rapidly from one to another, with Loeb, his secretary, coming in every few minutes with a telegram which Roosevelt would read and to which he would dictate an immediate reply.

Mr. Bacon turned to me and said, "Did you ever see such mental grasp?" Indeed I never had, and I think there are very few men who, like Roosevelt, could thoroughly grasp and quickly decide a problem, and immediately take up another. Roosevelt's ability as a statesman was, of course, only one phase of his dynamic, creative personality.

When the visitors had left, Roosevelt came over to us in his jolly, good-natured manner. That summer Roosevelt had killed a small black bear in the swamps of Mississippi. I told him I had just returned from Alaska, so he immediately asked me if I had killed any bears.

"Yes," I replied, "a Kodiak bear."

"You did! How large was he?"

"About twelve feet long, weighing, I should say, about fifteen hundred pounds."

"Bob," said Roosevelt, turning to Mr. Bacon, "that bear could have swallowed the one I killed in Mississippi like a pill and would never have known he had it inside of him."

CHAPTER XXV

PALETTE RANCH

THE Palette Ranch is to me one of the most delightful places in the world, beautifully situated in a valley at an altitude of seven thousand six hundred and fifty feet. It is surrounded by high mountains that stretch up into the ethereal blue to a height of thirteen or fourteen thousand feet, some of them perpetually covered with snow. I am almost tempted to write a description of this view but will not. While there is probably nothing more inspiring to gaze at than beautiful scenery, yet there is nothing more tiresome to read than a description of it. When you leave the noisy, busy throngs of New York, where everything is synthetic from its joy to its gin, and reach this high, remote spot, far removed from the racket of radios and rivets, it seems as if all cares, jealousies, and animosities of life have fallen from you. You have reached a higher altitude and a bigger world, and feel nearer heaven than ever before. Sometimes you feel as if you had wandered into a new dimension, where you might meet yourself.

When contemplating the beautiful mountains surrounding my ranch, the following lines occurred to me:

> Oh, mountains, my wonderful mountains,
> With the billowy clouds on your breast,
> With the sun on your lakes and your fountains,
> And your streams that are never at rest,

FROM A PAINTING OF MY RANCH IN WYOMING

From your crags where the eagles are screaming,
From your loftiest summits of snow,
My soul ascends in its dreaming,
To heights that I never may know.

The Rocky Mountain scenery, with its glorious purples, reds, and grays, is far more beautiful than that of Switzerland, with its hard blues, whites, and greens. No matter how carefully a Swiss scene is painted, the result looks like a stage-setting. On the other hand, a reproduction of a Rocky Mountain view may be truly lifelike, warm, and colorful.

The summer climate at my ranch is perfect. The temperature is never above sixty, and every night you sleep under two or three blankets. Surely there is no spot in the world where you get purer air and purer water, two very desirable elements in life, than at the Palette Ranch. When I first went there one could hang the quarter of an elk in a tree and it would dry before it would rot, the air was so free from microbes. Man may pat himself on the back for the wonderful scientific progress he has made. He may boast of the hospitals he has built, but he should remember that he also carries with him the microbes that fill these hospitals with patients.

At Palette Ranch, there is never a day when there is not sunshine. The nights are glorious in that clear atmosphere, for the stars, instead of being far-away points of light in the terrifying space beyond the world, are magnificent in their brightness as they continue their course of perpetual motion and perpetual silence. The moon is often so bright one can see to read by it.

Speaking of stars reminds me of an incident that occurred in my family. I have a nephew, Tiffany Richardson, who was born and brought up in New York. He was always put to bed at an early hour and had thus never seen the broad expanse of a starlit night, until he went to visit my father in the country. They called on a neighbor and remained for supper, not returning until after dark. Driving in an open carriage along the country road, little Tiffany had an expansive view of the sky on a clear and beautiful night. He was greatly impressed, asking my father all sorts of questions about the stars, and in turn father dilated on the beauties of God's creations. That night when little Tiffany knelt down to say his prayers, he ended up by saying, "I thank Thee, O God, for making such a lovely world, and putting such a beautiful top on it!"

How delightfully children sometimes say things! A little girl who had gone to church for the first time was asked on her return what the minister had said, and what his text had been. She thought for a while, and then said, "Keep your soul on top." None of the others could recall that text, but they found later the minister had preached from the text of St. Paul's, "Keep your body under." It was put in a better way by the little girl; if you keep your soul on top you need not trouble yourself about mortifying your body.

One day in Paris a lady introduced me to her little daughter, saying, "Mr. Anderson is an artist and paints pictures."

Little Marion asked, "Do you paint people or farms, Mr. Anderson?" meaning did I paint figures or landscapes.

There is no spot in the world where time passes more swiftly than at the ranch. When I have been there for three months, it seems no longer than three weeks, as there is always plenty to do. A golf course and swimming pool have been built for one's pleasure, or one can take a horseback ride every day for thirty days, each one of them beautiful, and never ride twice over the same trail.

There is probably not another ranch in the United States where better fishing and hunting, both birds and large game, may be found.

My log ranch house contains a combined living-dining room twenty feet square and twenty feet high. At one side is a huge fireplace which will take four-foot logs. To build the fireplace and chimney, which, as well as most of the house itself, is my own handiwork, forty four-horse wagonloads of stone had to be hauled four miles. I could not even procure a nail without sending to Billings, one hundred and fifty miles distant. I had no lime for mortar but found in the mountains a deposit of gypsum, which when burned and mixed with wood ashes, made an excellent mortar. The east and west wings contain bedrooms. To the north is the kitchen and servants' rooms, and to the south over the porte cochère is a sun-parlor opening from my office. The house as here described is of course the result of many years' work and was rebuilt after the fire.

We have at the ranch the most perfect summer climate in the United States, never a hot day and no fog. There is not a day the sun does not shine, at least, a part of the time. Anyone who has visited this ranch will never forget the blue, golden days of Wyoming.

There are only three species of trees that grow in that part of the Rockies, the conifer, the cottonwood, and the quaking asp. The tree of the quickest growth requires six weeks to form a ring, and unless it has this length of time to grow before frost, it cannot survive. Therefore, trees like the oak and others that require a longer time to form a ring cannot live at that altitude. The pine is one of our noblest and most impressive trees, standing upright and erect, reaching far up into the sky, and in its dignity resembling a church spire. Even when thrown prostrate to the ground by the storm, as long as it contains any life its point will turn upward and grow again toward the sky, showing still some thought of heaven in its heart.

The leaves of the quaking asp are at the end of a long stem and are constantly in motion, no matter how slight the breeze is. There is a legend concerning the quaking asp which says that the cross on which our Saviour was crucified was made from the wood of this tree and that this remembrance causes a constant quaking of its leaves.

There is no more nutritious grass in the world than the bunch or buffalo grass that covers the plains of Wyoming and among the fifteen hundred specimens of grass in the United States it is the oldest. Early in the spring, after the late snows have melted and moistened the ground, it begins to grow, and the spring rains soon make the verdure green and luxuriant. During the summer but little rain falls, however, so that by the end of June, cured by the sun, the grass becomes brown. It remains in that condition the rest of the year, and thus makes excellent grazing for the cattle, as it is almost as nutritious as oats. My horses roam at liberty in the open, and, without other food than the grass, remain fat all winter.

This is called bunch grass because it grows in bunches, and each bunch is more or less separated from the others. Sod, however, is a compact, continuous growth of grass, with intertwining roots, that only comes from cultivation, and except when cultivated is not found on our Western plains, the steppes of Russia, or the vast plains of Siberia. Probably three-fourths of the inhabitants of the earth have not seen sod.

I have tamed many wild animals on my ranch, and most interesting pets they are, far more intelligent than any domestic animal. One time I captured a small baby elk, carried it on the front of my saddle to the ranch and there played nurse to it. I brought that elk up on the bottle, and it thrived and grew, and became a great pet. It was very fond of me, following me wherever I went like a dog. When logs were being cut for my ranch house, the elk insisted on going with the men up into the mountains. The men were afraid a tree might fall and injure the elk, and, as there was no fence within which they could enclose it, they tried this scheme: in the morning, just before they were starting, they took a pan of oats, of which the elk was very fond, and placed it behind a small building. The elk remained to devour the oats, while they took the trail for the mountains. The next morning they tried the same trick. The elk took only one mouthful of oats, however, then came around the corner of the building, watched which direction they had taken, returned, ate his oats, and soon joined them. No cow would have had this amount of cunning.

At nighttime when I sat down beside a camp fire, the elk would sit down very near me, and, chewing its cud like an old-timer chewing tobacco, look meditatively into the fire.

This elk lived to be three years old and developed a fine pair of antlers. His death was particularly tragic and unnecessary. Rush had gone to a cabin on Jack Creek and the elk followed him. Rush entered a log house with some cronies (this was before the days of prohibition) and was having a convivial time drinking and playing cards with them. Fearing that the elk might wander away, he had tied one end of a rope to his horns and the other end of the rope to a tree. But instead of tying the elk closely to the tree, he stupidly tied him at the end of a long rope. The elk became frightened at something, ran, and suddenly reaching the end of the rope, received a jerk that broke his neck.

I have also had on my ranch tame deer, tame antelope, and, at one time, two large bull buffaloes that Colonel Cody had given me. Of all the pets I have had, the antelope, the most beautiful animal of the plains, is the most interesting. Within an enclosure at one time I raised seventeen elk, but as they were expensive to feed and I had no use for them, I turned them loose. They went to the head of Piney, where they summered and wintered and soon multiplied to nearly three hundred. In that locality, many of them are still to be found.

Distances in the West are very deceptive. Emerson Hough, the writer, who visited me at one time, had been admiring the pillar of beautifully colored sandstone which may be seen at the right of the picture of my ranch house. This pillar stands two hundred feet high and has resisted erosion because of a band of hard volcanic rock which caps it.

"Don't wait lunch for me, Colonel, if I am a little late," said Hough, as he set out with his kodak to photograph that prominent landmark.

I assented and smiled, but said nothing. I didn't wait lunch, and dinner time came. I ate alone. At nine-thirty Hough showed up, the weariest man I think I've ever seen. He had tramped miles to get to the pillar of sandstone and back.

From the range behind my ranch house on a clear day one can see the Big Horn Range, two hundred and fifty miles away, where for many years Roosevelt had his ranch.

CHAPTER XXVI

VISITORS AT THE RANCH

I HAVE had some pleasant experiences camping in the wildest parts of the Rockies with my congenial friend, Irving Bacheller. I have known him for many years, and to know him is to delight in him. We have had many interesting conversations late into the night beside our camp fires. A camp fire is one thing that is the same no matter in what part of the world you light it. I have lit my camp fire on the sands of the Libyan Desert, amid the dark canyons of the Rockies, and on the frozen snows of the Arctic where camp fires are as few and far between as the stars in the heavens. Wherever you light it, it crackles up with the same merry little flame, and like an old friend says: "Well! here I am again." I well remember sitting beside our camp fire enjoying its genial warmth and our cigars, while Irving told me many amusing stories. He is a famous raconteur. His stories are distinguished by vivid character drawing. This is one of them:

"I was on a stagecoach with our mutual friend, A. Barton Hepburn, crossing the sagebrush country from Kemmera to Cora, a distance of one hundred and ten miles. At Cora we were to meet our outfit and proceed in the saddle to Fish Creek Canyon. We had journeyed some thirty miles when a stout, cheerful woman got abroad, with a small bag in one hand, and a live hen in the other. Our driver, whose name was Romeo, helped her aboard. She sat at my side and told us the story of her life as we rode along. Her husband had been slain in a gun-fight years before, and she and her two daughters had kept the ranch going and made a success of it. The hen in her hands, its legs tied, seemed to be in disagreement with her as to certain details in the narrative.

" 'You shut up!' the woman would say. 'That's the brainiest hen in Wyoming. It's a caution to see her ketch grasshoppers. She'll git in the way they're travelin' an' take 'em comin' down like a man ketchin' a baseball. She's the best mother hen in Wyoming. She'll go right up in the air and fight it out with an owl or a hawk. She'll grab hold and hang on like a bulldog, and get meat and feathers every time. If a fox is around, seems so she could smell him, and she'll keep nigh the front door. Give her a flock o' chickens an' they'll git brought up proper an' have good manners. I've lent her all over the plains, an' I git ten cents a head fer every chicken she brings up. That's some hen, my son. Ye got to take yer hat off to her. If human bein's would send the good mothers around the state to bring up the children,—I mean them that know how,—we'd have better men an' women in Wyoming.'

"Here and there at the gate of some lonely ranch a girl would be waiting on a pony to take the mail from Romeo.

"Before the day ended, our cheery companion opened her bag and took out a box of black cigars, and having lighted one herself, offered them to the passengers.

"Next morning we got mired in a deep valley. It had rained in the night. Romeo could not start the mules. The woman, who sat next to me on the front seat with the driver, exclaimed,

" 'Lord Almighty! Ain't there any man here who can swear?'

PORTRAIT OF HON. EDWARD R. FINCH

"I had a week's growth of beard on my face and the passengers looked hopefully at me.

"Hepburn said with a smile, 'Bacheller, you try it.' To keep up the fun I tried it and thought I had made a fairly creditable effort.

"The woman said, 'Here, take this chicken!' and took the reins from my hands, saying, 'My God, boy, if ye talked that way to me I'd think ye were makin' love to me!'

"She cracked the whip and yelled. The yell was preceded by a loud remark calculated to remind the mules of disagreeable facts in the family history of each and every one of them. It seemed to be the kind of persuasion needed. Again we were on our way. She gave the reins to the driver and turned to me, saying: 'When ye're drivin' mules and are in this kind o' trouble here in Wyoming, boy, ye've got to know how to swear.' "

Bacheller's Western woman reminds me of another lady whom I heard about in California, a well-known character called Calamity Jane.

Calamity Jane brought suit for divorce against her husband.

"On what grounds," asked the judge, "do you bring suit for divorce?"

"Because my husband ran away and left me," Calamity Jane replied.

"And why," persisted the judge, "did your husband run away and leave you?"

"Because I was after him with an axe."

One summer Judge E. R. Finch of the New York Supreme Court Bench spent the summer at the ranch. At the same time Sidney Lenz was there. Lenz is beyond doubt the best bridge player in America; he can locate a card in any part of the pack, but when he gets in the open he can't even locate the sky.

Lenz, the Judge, and I went trout fishing one day down the Grey Bull River. A few miles below the ranch the river twists and winds through a deep canyon where there are many pools and trout in abundance. We rode down this canyon and commenced fishing. After a while the Judge and I fished upstream, losing sight of Lenz around a turn in the stream. We finally returned to the ranch without him. Although we knew of his difficulty in finding his way about, we were not anxious about him, since he had his horse with him. All he needed to do was to sit in the saddle and give the horse his head; he would be brought directly to the ranch. When it became dusk and he did not appear, however, I did become alarmed, and sent two cowboys in search of him. They rode down the river along the top of the canyon, and saw Lenz sitting on a rock beside the river where we had left him. One of the cowboys called down, "Lenz, are you lost?"

"No," Lenz replied, "I have a rendezvous with a young lady, and I am waiting here for her!"

The following summer I had as visitors at the ranch Wilbur Whitehead, Sidney Lenz, and Mrs. Jo Culbertson, who remained there most of the summer. They were three of the best card-players in the country, and we had bridge morning, noon, and night. At that time I was vice-president of the Knickerbocker Whist Club of New York, and greatly interested in the game of bridge, which, so far, is the most scientific game of cards that has been developed.

One summer I had a delightful visit from my friend Prince Albert of Monaco. He was seventy years of age, hale and hearty, a good sport, and an excellent shot and an

CRAYON DRAWING OF THE PRINCE OF MONACO
BY THE AUTHOR

enthusiastic hunter. I had invited him to the ranch as I felt sure that he would enjoy a sojourn in the Rockies.

He arrived with his suite, consisting of his doctor, his secretary, and his valet. He was most enthusiastic about the air and the surroundings of the ranch. We spent several days in fishing,—and the trout fishing there is unexcelled. We hunted birds, sage hens, and ruffed grouse; and then decided to make an excursion higher up in the mountains to hunt big game.

Assembling a camp outfit, we left the ranch with saddles and pack horses, and with my foreman, Rush, a horse-wrangler and a cook. We had been camping and hunting a few days in the mountains, when late one afternoon we were riding near the top of the divide which separates Grey Bull from Boulder Basin. Riding ahead and looking over the top of the ridge, I saw, a short distance beyond, a large mountain sheep, also called "bighorn."

We got off our horses, and I showed the Prince the mountain sheep. He had never killed one. Now was his chance. The sheep was only a few hundred yards distant, and the Prince could easily continue out of sight, along the ridge we were on, until he reached the point opposite the sheep. Then he would be but a short distance away and above his quarry, with the wind in his favor.

I remained to watch the sheep, and sent one of my men along to guide and help the Prince. At any moment I expected to hear a shot, but instead I saw the Prince returning, supported by the guide. The Prince, who was not accustomed to this high altitude (we were hunting at an altitude of over 11,000 feet) found that after proceeding a short distance he was unable to continue even with the help of a guide. The Prince was greatly disappointed not to have the horns of that sheep to add to his already valuable collection of animals.

We hunted a number of days just east of Yellowstone Park without seeing any game, but the Prince finally did bring down a fine bull elk, and also killed a bear. The skins of both of them I afterwards saw in his palace in Paris.

The Prince was not only a true sportsman but a delightful companion. He was highly educated and a scientist of some note. At that time he had written forty volumes on deep-sea soundings, and he was well informed on many other subjects. Although he was the owner of the Casino at Monte Carlo, he himself would not take liquor, or smoke, or touch a card. I regretted to say good-bye to him, but he was obliged to return to his principality. He evidently enjoyed his stay, to judge from the letter reproduced herewith, which I received from him.

When a few years later I was living in Paris, the Prince invited me to his palace for lunch. It was the last time I was to see him, for directly after lunch he was taken to the hospital for a serious operation, which he did not survive. His death was a loss to the scientific world, and I suffered the loss of a dear friend.

Though not by choice or design on my part, it has so happened that I have seen or met most of the crowned heads of Europe who were ruling during my lifetime. I occupied a box at the Crystal Palace, London, when in an adjoining box were gathered four famous rulers: Queen Victoria, Alexander II, Czar of Russia, Emperor William II, and the Shah of Persia.

I saw Emperor William II on one other occasion. I happened to be in Munich in 1880 when King Ludwig of Bavaria committed suicide by drowning. I was staying at the house of a colonel of the army who had charge of the funeral arrangements. He took me into the room where the king lay in state, and later I attended the funeral. Emperor

DRAWING OF EMPRESS EUGÉNIE OF FRANCE BY AUTHOR

William I and his son, then the Crown Prince, the last Kaiser of Germany, were in attendance at the funeral. I afterwards rode on the same train with them from Munich to Berlin.

It was my honor to attend a reception at the Royal Palace in Madrid many years ago, and there met the beautiful Queen Mercedes and the King, whose son, King Alfonso, was recently exiled from Spain. It has been my pleasure to meet King Victor Emmanuel of Italy and the Mikado of Japan. I also met King Edward VII of England on more than one occasion; the last time I saw King Edward, he was lunching in a garden at Marienbad with Maxine Elliott.

At Granada I was once making a sketch in the Alhambra when an elderly lady accompanied by several pretty girls, stopped by my easel.

"It is very pretty—what you make," the elderly lady remarked. We conversed for several minutes before she and her party withdrew. A Spanish soldier on guard then came up to me and inquired, "Do you know who that is?" I replied that I did not.

"It is the ex-Empress Eugénie of France."

Had I known to whom I was talking, I would have told her that one of my very early efforts, before I had studied art, was a drawing of her face. This early drawing can be seen in the following illustration.

But this catalogue of royalty is significant only on account of the rather startling fact that they have all reigned and disappeared within my lifetime. One question naturally arises: Is the world better off for the change from monarchy to democracy? One thing is apparent: the world is losing its sense of reverence. Children no longer revere their parents. Authority in moral and social, as well as in political, realms is lessening. When a nation was ruled by a king, the people naturally looked up to him as the head of the

Paris Nov. 21st of 1913

Dear Mr Anderson,

I have now settled again at home and I want to tell you how often, how much I am thinking of the happy days that I spent with you in that country where you did everything to turn it out as a paradise for me. Though I did much sporting life during half a century, every hour that I had in the Rockies will remain in my memory under a shining light. Of course my gratefulness to you stands high over my other feelings. What a happy dream it would be for me if I could renew such a pleasure!

And not only have I enjoyed that fine sport in admirable forests and high altitudes, but during the following weeks my satisfaction was completed with a series of uninterrupted surprises in my experience

of American work and scientific progress.
Fortunately, I had the seven days confinement on board to think quietly over
the many roads along which this happy
ocean had taken me. And now, very
often still, my thoughts fly over that
country where our footprints lie under
the snow.

And now, sum Mr. Anderson, wishing
to see you some day in my own
country or at least in France, I beg
you to offer my best compliments to
Mrs. Anderson and to consider me
as a very sincere friend.

Albert, Pce of Monaco

State and as the one of supreme authority. It was then easier for them to raise their thoughts to a Heavenly King. Russia shot its Czar and now the nation says, "There is no Heavenly King."

The last king will probably sit on the English throne. Owing to their extreme conservatism, it is said that an Englishman will not look at the new moon out of his respect for the old. When all other nations have become republics and their crowns, jewels, and throne-chairs, with their glory and gold and glitter, have been relegated to museums, England will still sail on in an even keel with the figurehead of a king on the prow.

A DAY AT THE RANCH

Saddle Star Valley! Hey, feller, be quick!
 I'll jump on his back for a ride up "the crick,"
With "slicker" on saddle and gun by my side,
 We'll ride up the valley, ride, ride, ride, and ride,
Free as the air, or the breezes to blow,
 We have not a care, nor a sorrow we know.
I will show you a pool in a shadowy dell,
 Where the trout are as thick as the sinners in Hell.

There is a place they are jumping about,
 You throw in your line and you yank out a trout;
Just a few casts and you have quite enough,
 For your creel is as full as a "feller" can stuff.
And then for a smoke and a full hour of ease,
 Lazily stretched in the shade of the trees,
Watching the cook assaulting the "chuck"
 And swapping big lies about fisherman's luck.

Gazing at sparks as they gracefully rise,
 Blending at last with the blue of the skies.
Oh, blessed is the cook and the bacon he fries.
 The smoke and the smell will bring tears to your eyes.
We'll eat and we'll eat till we're ready to burst
 And in the spring water, we'll slacken our thirst.

Then flat on backs, breathing big heaves,
   We'll snooze for a while in the needles and leaves,
And the problems of life will no longer survive:
   They are lost in the thought that the heart is alive.
We have fished. We have feasted and drifted away;
   But the lengthening shadows have told that the day
Goes like the dreams that have glittered and passed.
   Our playtime in daytime is over at last.
We mount our brave steeds and homeward we ride
   Over the trails of the steep mountainside.

We are thrilled by the picture the high heavens hold
   Of cloudland refulgent with crimson and gold,
And we watch the steep canyon grow darker and fill,
   With purple as deep as the far distant hill,
The somber expression of oncoming night,
   Draped at the base of a mountain peak, white,
That rising above the surrounding haze
   Receives a bright kiss from the sun's last rays.

The mantle of night on the countryside falls.
   Away in a valley, the coyote calls.
Blindly, the ponies cling close to the track
   Of the light on the window-sill, luring us back.
The pleasures of daytime have taken their flight,
   And tired, but happy, we bid you good-night.

PART
FIVE

CHAPTER XXVII

MRS. ANDERSON

In 1921 I suffered the loss of my wife, a noble woman whose entire life was devoted to helping others and to works of public philanthropy. Being a woman of positive character, she naturally encountered differences of opinion, but she had the love and respect of all who knew her. Her every act was inspired by unselfish and noble motives.

The daughter of the late Jeremiah and Elizabeth Lake Milbank, she first entered the field of public service as a friend of the higher education of woman. In 1894, when Barnard College was struggling for a footing among the women's colleges of the country, she became a trustee and two years later became chairman of the board, and gave the administration building on 119th Street, known as Milbank Hall. Still later, in 1903, Mrs. Anderson, realizing that the future of Barnard depended upon the control of sufficient property to permit of expansion, purchased at a cost of a million dollars the three city blocks bounded by 116th and 119th Streets west of Broadway and gave to the college the site which has made its development possible. During her lifetime Mrs. Anderson provided not only financial support to Barnard, but also wise and farsighted counsel and personal friendship to many individual students. Without her aid, Barnard College could scarcely have come to occupy its position in the educational life of the nation.

In 1904, Mrs. Anderson first entered the field of public

health. At this early stage, she recognized that sickness is a major factor in poverty and that an unwholesome environment is, in turn, a fertile cause of sickness. Her attention was called to conditions in the lower East Side of New York where she saw crowded tenements and unsanitary streets swarming with dirty children. She gave to the New York Association for Improving the Condition of the Poor funds for the erection of the Milbank Public Baths on East Thirty-eighth Street, which was a building so perfect in design and operation that it served as a model for the series of public baths subsequently developed under municipal auspices.

In 1909, Mrs. Anderson gave to the Children's Aid Society the land and buildings for the Home for Convalescent Children at Chappaqua, New York, to which are sent each year children from the poor sections of New York City who are suffering from the after-effects of serious illness. Here, about an hour's ride from the city, in a cluster of attractive buildings surrounded by spreading lawns, thousands of waifs from the city tenements have found health and happiness.

During the Great War she gave unstintedly to relief and welfare organizations, and she purchased and sent continuously through her own organization tons of food and medical supplies regularly for several years, to aid the suffering people of Belgium and France. After the armistice, she made it possible for the Memorial Fund Association to give largely to the sick and destitute children of Serbia, and to the starving children of Central Europe. In recognition of her service to France, she was created by the government in 1918 a chevalier of the Legion of Honor.

At the time of Mrs. Anderson's death, I received the following letter from the French Government, showing its deep appreciation for Mrs. Anderson's generous aid given to the French soldiers:

RÉPUBLIQUE FRANÇAISE

Ministère
des
Affaires étrangères

Paris, le Ier Juillet 1921.

Direction des Affaires
administrative et techniques

Tous Direction
Des Affaires Administratives
& Des Union Internationales

MONSIEUR ANDERSON:

Mme. GRIGGS, Présidente du "Trait d'Union Franco-Américaine," m'avait fait connître, à plusieurs reprises, l'importance de la coopération qu'apportait à cette d'oeuvre Madame ANDERSON, tant par ses dons personnels que par l'activé propagande qu'elle ne cessait de faire aux États-Unis en faveur de la France, et en particulier de nos régions dévastées.

Aussi c'est avec un profond regret que j'ai appris sa mort prématurée, survenue avant que les circonstances m'aient permis de lui addresser un témoignage officiel de la gratidude du Gouvernement français.

Je tiens du moins à vous assurer, en vous exprimant mes sincères condoléances, que l'oeuvre bienfaisante accomplie par Madame ANDERSON a été hautement appréciée en France.

Veuillez agréer, Monsieur, l'assurance, de ma haute considération.

Pour le Ministre et par son ordre
LE DIRECTEUR DES AFFAIRES ADMINISTRATIVES
ET TECHNIQUES

Maurice Herbette

In the beautiful chapel of Princeton College Mrs. Anderson built a choir of rare loveliness and dignity. Speaking at the dedication, Mr. Albert G. Milbank said of Mrs. Anderson, "High spirited and vivid in every thought and word, radiating a charm that cast its spell over all who come in contact with her, she devoted her energies and her resources to a life of service. In fact, her benefactions were so noble it was said of her at the time of her death that, had she lived in the Middle Ages, she would have been canonized and known as 'Saint Elizabeth,' and yet, saint though she was, those of us who knew her best hold her in affectionate remembrance quite as much for her occasional fallibility, her humor, and those endearing human qualities which made her a woman."

CHAPTER XXVIII

MY DAUGHTER AND THE JUDSON
HEALTH CENTER

I HAVE but one child, Dr. Eleanor Anderson Campbell. Eleanor was graduated at the Spence School, went to Bryn Mawr College, and then entered the Boston University School of Medicine from which she was graduated with high honors, being the only student, male or female, in her class to receive *cum laude*. She did not seek the degree of M.D. with the idea of being a general practitioner. The desire of her heart was to aid the sick children among the poor families of New York. She therefore specialized in pediatrics. Her first intention was to found a children's hospital in New York, but on further investigation she decided a health center, properly organized, would be of greater benefit.

After canvassing various parts of New York, she found, just south of the Washington Arch, a part of Greenwich Village where dreadful conditions existed. Crowded in twenty blocks were 45,000 people, mostly Italians, an average of 1,600 people to a block. Once a district of dignified homes, it had degenerated into a run-down, dilapidated, poverty-stricken neighborhood, with wretched housing conditions.

Visiting these people in their crowded tenement homes, one came away, as my daughter often told me, with the feeling that life, perforce, must have been a continued tragedy for such of them as had been compelled by circumstances to exchange a home in one of Italy's sunny hamlets for the congestion and squalor of a New York tenement section. Small wonder these people succumb so quickly to disease and that their children, unless taken early in hand and trained in habits of health and hygiene, become the undeveloped, malnourished youths so typical of this and other congested tenement areas of the larger centers of population. In these miserable, dilapidated tenement houses, ill ventilated, well nigh sunless, and living in three-room apartments will often be found from three to twelve individuals.

Daily encountering these sordid conditions, my daughter decided to devote her life and means to ministering to the health and social needs of the sorely afflicted people of this community, and, accordingly, founded the Judson Health Center which has since become known throughout the area as a Human Repair Shop. To it come daily hundreds of poor, tired, poverty-tried mothers with their sick children, seeking relief from physical ills. With the aid of a trained staff of physicians and nurses, Dr. Campbell has succeeded in winning back to health thousands of little ones who otherwise would have gone to join the already large army of malnourished tenement children, eventually to become physically handicapped citizens. For these children, a health center such as that established by my daughter is a vital necessity.

It is always interesting to hear Dr. Campbell tell of the peculiar conditions she has had to meet and overcome in her health work among these people. In health work among the foreign-born, the Judson Health Center clinics frequently experience considerable difficulty in meeting and overcoming their native superstitions, customs, and traditions. Some of these age-old traditions are so deeply a part of the lives of these people that, in cases where modern medical science might intervene to good advantage, the Center finds itself backed up against a solid blank wall, impossible to penetrate. To such people, radium, X-ray, surgery, diet, and hygiene seem worlds away; and strike them as drab and unromantic. One such age-old tradition encountered by Dr. Campbell's nurses is that relating to the cure of an abscess through the medium of a charm. In such cases, some sort of inscription is marked on the swollen area and an incantation (only used when the moon is in a certain quarter) is recited by someone bearing special credentials. This is expected to cure the abscess.

To obtain a real picture of the service rendered by the community center operated by Dr. Campbell, one must know the mothers, the love they bear their children, and the hope they have for their future well-being, happiness, and prosperity. It is true these people are slow to learn new ways, and difficulty is experienced in overcoming their native superstitions, customs, and traditions. Yet, when they are reached through the child, their eagerness to learn what to do, and their perseverance in overcoming difficulties, will convince one that, after all, the job is worth while and that he has been well repaid for all the labor expended. Illustrative of these facts is the case of a little Italian woman, whose perseverance and pluck have been an inspiration to the health center workers. I shall tell the story as it came to me from Dr. Campbell.

This little Italian woman had eight children. When the family first came to the notice of one of Dr. Campbell's workers, the oldest boy was found sick and helpless abed; the three next were badly nourished, the fifth and sixth completely crippled, with legs bent through rickets to a letter "s," so that they could only stand on the outside of their feet when supported; and the two babies, aged one and two, were "four-plus ricket" cases, bent the same way. The four little children crawled around the floor, unattended and unguarded. The father was at work in a factory, and the mother had gone out to visit a "faith doctor."

"For," said the hopelessly crippled and bed-ridden lad, "they say she cures you, and I begged my mother to go and find her, and ask her to pray for me, so I can get some strength in my legs. Maybe she can make me walk."

Once acquainted with the nurse that Dr. Campbell sent to the home, the mother responded by bringing first one child and then another to the clinic. The older children had gone so long without care that it was practically impossible to help them, but the doctors and nurses undertook to help Carmella, Louis, Anna, and Rose. Carmella and Louis, five and four years old, could only be helped by serious orthopedic operations. With touching confidence, the father and mother sent their little girl to undergo the ordeal.

Louis was also unable to walk. His legs, however, did not look so bad as those of Carmella, so the parents could not be induced at first to let him be operated upon. Dr. Campbell, not believing in coercion, decided to have Louis taken into the Health Nursery operated in connection with the clinic, so that he might be built up, postponing to another date any talk of his operation, which was later accomplished. The babies, Anna and Rose, were also admitted to the nursery.

At this a new difficulty presented itself. How could the mother bring the three helpless little ones to the clinic? The Association for the Aid of Crippled Children became interested in the problem, a baby carriage was donated, and with its aid the mother began her part in effecting the cure. Every day, after getting the older children off to school, this brave little woman washed and dressed the three cripples, carried each one down two flights of tenement stairs, and brought them to the Center Nursery. Each week she attended the mothers' class; morning and evening she listened to the suggestions of the nurse; at times she reported to the clinic and heard the advice of the doctors. At home she cooked cereals, prepared vegetables, and followed the other dietary instructions given her. She did her part, and did it well.

The conditions of the children steadily improved from the time they entered the nursery. The babies, Rose and Anna, developed into sturdy, normal youngsters. Louis and Carmella had their deformities remedied by operations. So all were able to attend school and to participate like normal children in school activities. Judson continued to watch over those children until they had reached the stage where they could be discharged with safety from an exacting and intensive form of supervision.

The growth of the work of the Judson Health Center has been quite remarkable. From a lowly beginning with a few employees, the center constantly has expanded and widened the sphere of its influence until, today, it has come to be recognized as among the largest and most efficiently operated health educational agencies in the country.

The organization's growth and immense success, the saving of lives of thousands of children, is chiefly owing to my daughter's inspiration, vision, and work, as she not only is the head of all medical work but through her efforts the yearly budget of $100,000 is raised.

CHAPTER XXIX

BETTY

My daughter Eleanor had but one child, a little girl by the name of Betty, as sweet and pretty a child as ever was born. She never had an awkward age, and was graceful and beautiful from childhood up. She grew to be tall and stately with a handsome figure and an exceedingly beautiful face. She had a most winning smile, a magic smile, which from rosy childhood flushed her face. I wrote some verses about Betty's smile, one of which I remember as follows:

> When kindly God our Betty made
> He looked at her awhile,
> And then He added one more charm,
> He taught her how to smile.

Betty was very fond of the West and spent several summers at my ranch. She was an excellent horsewoman and an enthusiastic fisherman; so we spent many happy hours riding, hunting, and fishing among the streams of that delightful region.

We lived together as close companions during her entire life, and in all that time I never heard her say or knew her to do a thing that ought not to have been said or done. I never once heard her raise her voice in anger, or make an unkind remark to anyone or about anyone.

She was graduated at the Spence School and then went to Wellesley College. During her second year she became acquainted with Mr. Henry Adams Ashforth, who appeared to be more attractive to her than her studies. She became

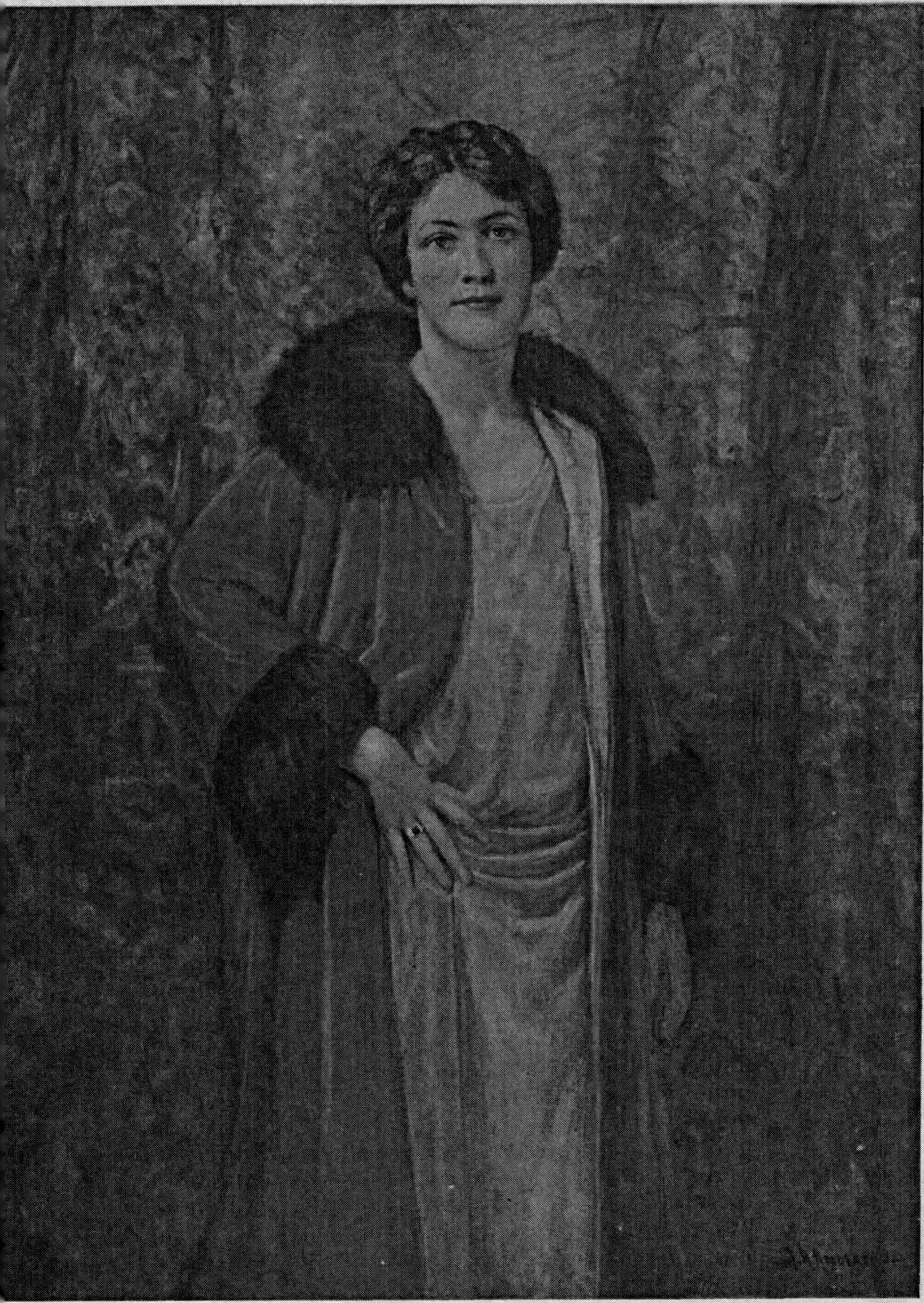

PORTRAIT OF BETTY

engaged to him at the end of her second year in college. As Mr. Ashforth was an unusually fine young man, the family raised no objection, and instead of returning to college, she was joined in the holy bonds of matrimony to Mr. Ashforth. There probably never was a more happy and perfectly congenial couple, and they had five years of married life as full of joy as often comes to mortals. They were literally one.

Before leaving New York for a short stay in Florida, I said good-bye to Betty, my only grandchild. She was in glorious health, and as happy as the day was long. I had been in Florida but a short time when I received a telegram saying that Betty was ill. I took the first train back to New York, and on arriving at the hospital found Betty very ill indeed. She was suffering from a streptococcic infection. The care of the most capable physicians, the best scientific knowledge and attention, were of no avail. Her death was so sudden that it doesn't yet seem real. It seems like some frightful nightmare, from which I will awaken to find it only a dream. But I know that it is real; I shall always be haunted by the thought that I shall never see Betty again.

Just before dying, she called her husband to the bedside, and putting her arms around his neck, whispered in his ear, "Oh, Ad, isn't it beautiful?"

If there is a beautiful spot in Paradise, Betty deserves it.

Betty left two lovely children, Ellie and Henry. A lamentable fact connected with this tragedy is that they will never know how glorious a mother they lost.

The following lines which I wrote the morning of her funeral were read at the service:

We think of Betty as being here;
Wherever we are, we feel her near,
In the busy moment, in the hushed hour,
We think of her as love's white flower.

The pressure of her hand we may not feel,
But over our spirits there still will steal
A mystic light, a loving thought,
Such as her presence always brought.

Of my life she is still a part,
And from her place within my heart
She'll guide my steps to the very end,
My truest, best and dearest friend.

PORTRAIT OF ELLIE AND HENRY ASHFORTH BY THE AUTHOR

CHAPTER XXX

CONCLUSION

As my last illustration I will introduce my latest picture, which I have just completed.

I had just been reading George Sand's "Lélia," in which she tells of Lélia taking the veil, and one day, seated alone in my studio after lunch, indulging in a pipe dream and looking at the sixteenth-century doorway that adorns my studio, this vision appeared before me. I saw Lélia, robed in white, coming through the open doorway with an exalted expression on her face as though she were looking into another world, a little girl on either side with a white candle in her hand and a little light dancing on top like a star dropped from heaven.

I took a piece of white canvas and half a dozen earthly colors, and with these materials I reproduced on canvas my vision, so that it perhaps might endure for hundreds of years. It is interesting to visualize a vision, so that it is visible to others.

The most important and most difficult things to obtain in any painting are the three subtle things in nature: life, light, and atmosphere. In reproducing a painting by mechanical means it is difficult to reproduce the atmosphere of the picture. A picture appeals to the emotions and to the intellect. Color is sensuous and appeals to the emotions, while the drawing, composition, chiaroscuro, and the story that it tells appeal to the mind; and a picture, to be complete, should contain all of these elements.

235

In the foregoing pages I have spoken of some of the events of my life as they recurred to me, and I hope that they will have proved of some interest to my readers. May I be allowed to close with a few reflections on my general outlook on life?

We live in a world governed by immutable laws. Therefore this rule is fundamental: if we break the laws of nature, the laws of nature will break us. It behooves us to acquaint ourselves with the laws of nature and live accordingly, and not be governed by the blind superstition that, if we ask God, he will change these laws for our personal benefit. In this world every cause has an effect and every effect has a cause. If a young man is born with two qualities, namely, energy and curiosity, curiosity to want to know and energy to find out, he will learn a lot during his earthly transit.

During the many years that I have wandered over the face of the earth, I have seen many changes brought about by man's science and inventive genius, whereby machinery has replaced hand labor in caring for human needs. The numerous inventions that have changed the entire history of mechanics and human welfare had their commencement during and since the Civil War. Necessity is the mother of invention. During that great conflict, when the men of the North were drafted into the army and the cultivation of the farms was left largely to the women and children, the government was faced with a shortage of wheat to feed its army. Up to that time man had broken the soil with a wooden plough, practically the same instrument that was used by the Romans in the time of the Caesars; in reaping he used a hand sickle similar to that used in Egypt in the time of the Pharaohs. At this juncture, however, when famine threatened us, Deering perfected the modern steel plough, and McCormick invented the reaper and the threshing machine, a machine that could clean seven hundred and forty

FROM A PAINTING OF LÉLIA TAKING THE VEIL

litres of wheat in the same time as the implement, the flail, would clean sixty. At the close of the war the nation not only had abundance of food for the army but, for the first time, was exporting wheat to Europe.

These and other mechanical improvements have not only changed our mode of living but have influenced our mental outlook. The perfecting of the telescope has brought the heavens nearer, and the telegraph and the radio have made all men neighbors. When Lincoln delivered his first inaugural address at Washington, it was telegraphed to St. Louis and was transported from there to San Francisco by the Pony Express. Today the words spoken by the President in Washington can be heard almost instantly, not only in San Francisco, but in farther parts of the world.

It is easy, however, to overestimate the importance of mechanical invention and the so-called wonders of modern science. I have already spoken of the intelligence of ants. There is a race of ants in Africa, a very small ant that builds his house by taking a certain kind of earth, mixing it with saliva and forming cement. Thus they have been known to build a house twenty-five feet in height and so hard it cannot be destroyed by a rhinoceros horn. The interior is beautifully arranged with columns and galleries, and in the center of this house the ants prepare room for a species of larva that lays all their eggs. There is also a central heat, from what cause nobody knows, but a central point is always much warmer than any other. New Yorkers glory in their sky-scrapers, but should man build a house in proportion to his height as this to the ants it would be two and a half miles high!

There is a race of ants in Brazil that will build a house in the trees, so constructed as to be impervious to the tropical rains. On the floor of this small house, they prepare soil and plant flowers. There are other ants that, by chewing leaves, make an emulsion and prepare the ground in which they sow a variety of fungus which they eat. Another type of ants are cowboys. When milking time comes, they will drive a flock of plant lice (aphids) over the leaves and, by rubbing their sides with the antennae, cause them to give forth a drop of white liquid called honeydew which they eagerly devour.

The aphids do not bite off pieces of leaf and swallow them, but are suction insects and live on the juice of plants. Another strange thing about the aphids is that a colony will be composed exclusively of female aphids, a quite perfect little suffragist paradise; in the tropical regions, they remain entirely female, but in the northern climate, where the aphids are killed by frost during the winter, they produce a certain number of males, in some mysterious way, in the month of October. The aphid has been viviparous up to that time, but now become oviparous and lays a fertilized egg on a twig of an apple tree just below where the first leaves will appear in the spring; these eggs hatch out and the insects commence at once to devour the leaves and, unless the tree is sprayed, will kill the tree.

There is a race of ants in Africa that will kill elephants. They are apparently always on the march, and there are millions of them. When they attack an elephant they get in his trunk, and as a matter of fact completely cover him. The elephant can save his life only by rushing into water deep enough to submerge himself. If there is no water near by he is known to have been killed by these ants. They swarm up his nose and over every part of his body, and their jaws are strong enough to cut through his tough hide and devour the carcass. These ants, however, cannot endure the heat of Africa's sun. They will always be found accompanied by another race of ants, small brown ones, which form a line on either side of the main body, and their marching is usually done at night or through the dense shade of the jungle. And when they are obliged to pass an open spot where the sun is shining, these brown ants form a tunnel, so that the black ants can march in the shade. There are other races of ants that have trained armies which battle for them.

To prove that the ant is not guided by instinct alone but by reason (although it is difficult to decide the point where instinct leaves off and reason begins), a scientist one time placed a piece of camphor in a nest built by ants. When the ants returned, there was immediate confusion, as all insects detest the odor of camphor. After a consultation, the ants proceeded to roll the camphor out through the door, but they found the opening too small. They rolled it back, enlarged the opening, and rolled the camphor out, thus solving by their reason a problem that had never before confronted them. The brain of an ant is encased in its shining little head, about half the size of a pinhead and almost negligible in comparison with the 1400 grammes of gray matter in the human skull.

I have never been a very strong believer in the doctrine of evolution. It is so much easier to go down than to go up, and the primitive races we speak about are more likely to be the degenerate end of a once civilized race than the commencement of a new one. A man or a race can only develop the inherent germ that is within him, and having reached the highest point of development he begins to decline.

One of the oldest races with which we are familiar today is the Berber race, inhabiting the north coast of Africa. They have been there since time immemorial, and have come in contact with all the highest civilizations in the world—the Phoenicians, the Arabs, and the Romans. In 1830 their country was invaded and taken possession of

A few scientists, however, think it was by direct collision with another body that the planets were formed. Whether produced by direct collision or tidal effect, it is an accident which would probably not be a frequent occurrence, and therefore, of the hundreds of millions of stars in the sky, but very few probably have planetary systems. When a planet is formed, it commences cooling off. Water and land appear and from some mysterious source, when it is sufficiently cooled and when a certain combination occurs of organic atoms, life emerges. The cooling off continues and in time the planet will be uninhabitable; then a barren, frozen region will continue to revolve through space. The whys and wherefores we can never know, as a finite mind cannot comprehend the Infinite.

Even planets are not very hospitable. In our solar system there are nine planets, and apparently the earth is the only planet on which life as we know it can exist. The planet nearest the sun, Mercury, always exposes the same side turned to the sun, just as the moon has the same side turned towards the earth. This side of Mercury is hotter than boiling water. The opposite side is without light and is intensely cold.

Venus is constantly surrounded by a dense vapor. This is not clouds of watery vapor such as we know, but probably dicarbon or some other gas. As it contains no oxygen, there is probably no vegetable life on Venus. On the earth, our principal supply of oxygen is given out from the vegetable growth.

Our nearest neighbor on the other side is Mars, a little brother only half of our diameter. Some scientists think there is a possibility of life on Mars, but not a probability, on account of the intense cold. Beyond Mars is a planet so far removed from the sun that its temperature is 270 degrees below zero Fahrenheit; even more intense cold prevails on those planets which are farther removed from the sun.

In the light of these facts, it appears that life as we know it is not the main object of creation. But while we are necessarily groping here amid many unknown facts, man has always been inspired in his endeavors by the grand hope of the soul's immortality, the hope that some day we shall know as we are known. We do know there is more than one kind of immortality: the immortality of the body which we transmit to our children; the immortality of the mind in a great work of art, literature, or musical composition; and, as we all hope, the immortality of the soul.

It is not likely that anyone living on the earth today will again see the changes that have occurred during the past thirty years.

At the beginning of the present century all the world was at peace and every nation was desirous of promoting the welfare of others. All was peace and tranquillity only disturbed by the occasional rattling of the Kaiser's sword in its scabbard. All the kings of Europe except Napoleon the Third were securely seated on their thrones. The aged Queen Victoria and the beautiful Queen Wilhelmina governed their nations, revered and loved by all their subjects. Lenin and Stalin had not been heard of.

Paris, the world's last art center, was at its apogee. Great sculptors, painters, writers, musical composers, actors and actresses there and in other cities raised the world to a high state of mentality.

Bright, gay, beautiful Paris was the Mecca of pleasure lovers from all parts of the world. Its boulevards thronged with promenaders and many, seated at the tables in front of the restaurants, were engaged in animated conversations or quietly sipping their wine.

Beautiful women, beautifully dressed, seated in open calèches, drove among the chestnut trees of the Champs Élysées in full flower.

Cavaliers and ladies on horseback rode the bridle paths of the Bois under the tender green of its trees. Lovers also were there seated in fiacres with the top up, and from the shadows sounds of kisses might be heard. All the world, feeling secure, was lost in a dream of happiness. Millionaires in America were building palaces and filling them with works of art.

Then came the World War which, like a cyclone, swept over the earth, leaving only death and destruction in its wake. Man used all his intellect, skill, and inventiveness in mechanics and chemistry to devise means of killing his fellow man, and nine million men were wiped out, were thrown like sticks on the fire to be consumed.

Now the wonderful edifice of civilization that mankind had taken centuries to erect with such infinite pains has crumbled and fallen to the ground. The inhabitants are groping about amid the ruins vainly looking for some faint ray of light and not knowing which way to turn.

As the world seems now to be headed toward socialism it may take centuries before we can again attain the high peak of refinement, culture, and civilization that the world knew in 1900. At the same time:

> In the darkest night of the year
> When all the stars have gone out,
> Courage is better than fear
> And faith is better than doubt.

And now, dear reader, since the best of friends must part, I will say good-bye.

In wandering together over the highways and byways of my life, I hope we have found some points of mutual interest. I am sorry that this has been a monologue instead of a dialogue, so that I might have heard the sound of your voice. Doubtless you could have suggested many improvements, but an autobiography is like a radio: you cannot talk back. Perhaps some time our trails may cross. Until then, dear reader, adios.

CPSIA information can be obtained at www.ICGtesting.com
Printed in the USA
LVOW100551080812

293435LV00004B/13/P